Holiness, Faith & Purity

A 30-DAY DEVOTIONAL

Bishop Walter & Annette Hawkins

KINGDOM NEWS TODAY
Publication Services, LLC

HOLINESS, FAITH & PURITY:
A 30-DAY DEVOTIONAL

Authors: Bishop Walter and Annette Hawkins
Editor: Anjeanette Alexander
Publication Services (Cover & Interior Design) – Kingdom News Publication Services, LLC.

DISCLAIMER
All the material contained in this book is provided for educational and informational purposes only. No responsibility can be taken for any results or outcomes resulting from the use of this material.

While every attempt has been made to provide information that is both accurate and effective, the author does not assume any responsibility for the accuracy or use/misuse of this information.

Printed in the United States of America.
ISBN 978-0692175026

U.S. Copyright Office
101 Independence Ave. S.E., Washington, D.C. 20559-6000

DEDICATION

We would like to dedicate this book to our children; Ericka Davis, Brian and Jordan Hawkins who were born in that order. They're all grown up and living their own lives.

They were typical children growing up in the small town of Carthage, AR and were fortunate to live in a small town without a lot of the problems children from larger cities often face. I remember the boys catching crawfish in mud puddles with their friends and catching fish that were not big enough to eat, while our daughter was into girly things.

Our children had a strong support system of spiritual leaders that they respected and listen to and for that we are thankful.

Ericka, Brian, and Jordan; Mom and Dad love you and that is why we choose to dedicate this book to the three of you. Next to God and one another, the three of you are a treasure given to us and we honor the Lord for the great memories both past and future that we will share with you and your families.

FOREWORD

It is with great honor and a privilege to have been asked to write this foreword on behalf of the new authors. In July 2017, I was in the same place that Bishop and Evangelist Hawkins are in right now of becoming an author. I am so happy for them as they stepped out on this journey and pray that they have great success sharing the Gospel in this format.

I love to see those who have received an assignment from the Lord and then walk boldly in their assignment, even if they don't feel fully equipped while walking it out. Often times as we step out, we have to learn new things so that new projects and assignments can properly be birthed.

I first met this lovely couple when our church visited Zion Hill Baptist Church in Camden, Arkansas in the later part of 2011. Not too long after meeting them at this meeting, Bishop Hawkins was invited to come speak at our church.

As time went on, there were several times when I have worked on various projects for First Missionary Baptist Church for both Bishop and Evangelist Hawkins. It is through these interactions that I learned the heart of this couple. They are extremely dedicated to the work of the Gospel while operating in great integrity. Both of them have a great passion to seeing people advance and develop in their gifts, talents and abilities. I also have learned that Evangelist Hawkins has a great sense of humor and even though she states she is not too tech savvy, she knows more than many others.

I have had the opportunity to read the devotionals within this book and know that those who read them and apply them to their lives will be completely blessed and have the opportunity to grow in their spiritual journey. The devotions cover a wide range of topics that tend to hinder the progression of God's people in the Kingdom. The pages of this book come from the heart of Bishop and Evangelist Hawkins, but it's through the unction and inspiration of the Holy Spirit that lives and resides within them that the words filled these pages.

It is my prayer that this project is just a stepping stone to many more for this power couple. I know that you as the readers will be blessed and know that God loves each of us so much and just desires to reward us with His riches and glory, but we have to do our part in drawing near to the all mighty God because He will always keep His word and draw nigh to us (James 4:8).

Erica McGraw, Author
Bryant, Arkansas

INTRODUCTION

It is with great excitement to present to each of you this literary work that the Lord has placed in our hearts for the people of God. In this 30-Day Devotional Book we have sought the Lord on the topics to share with His children and there has been much prayer concerning the words shared throughout the pages.

We have been working on this project for a while and did not say a word until the right time. We wanted to surprise those that are close to us with this assignment from the Lord. It was so hard to keep this surprise from those we love, but we know there will be a great reward in its completion.

We would like to introduce ourselves as just everyday people, living a simple but fulfilled life. We are Pastor and wife of First Missionary Baptist church, in the small town of Carthage, AR. We are the parents of three adult children as well as Mimi and Papa to four grandchildren. We have numerous spiritual children that we love so much.

Our mandate is to do the work of the Lord with excellence and excitement, preaching, teaching and evangelizing wherever we are sent. We've been pastoring for ten years, and God has blessed us to send five young pastors and wives out from First Baptist Church. It is the Lord's doing, and it is marvelous in our eyes to see the growth and development as well as the gifts and abilities that are being sharpened for the sake of the Kingdom.

ABOUT THE BOOK

Thank you for purchasing this devotional book. It is our prayer that it will help you in many areas in your walk with the Lord. It is our vision that this book be used for your morning devotional time with the Lord. We see people up early in the morning with their cup of coffee, reading these short devotionals and then reflecting on the Word. Just spending quiet time alone with the Lord to reflect on His Word.

As we began to think about the design of the book, the vision of a calla lily came to mind. Then we found some information about the meaning of a calla lily and what it represents. It has been depicted with the Virgin Mary or an Angel of Annunciation similar to the visitation of the angel Gabriel to Mary as shared in Luke 1:26-38.

In Greek, the name calla lily is the word for beautiful. The most common meaning is purity, holiness, and faithfulness and that is how we determined the name of Holiness, Faith & Purity, A 30-Day Devotional.

As many may know, the calla lily is a popular flower used during the time we celebrate the resurrection of Christ. It is used as a symbol for rebirth and resurrection, which is tied to the resurrection of Jesus because they are shaped like trumpets which symbolize triumph and victory. When we are in Christ Jesus, we are victorious and triumphant in all things.

There is a place after each entry for you to reflect on the Word. The oil lamp on the reflection page serves to remind us that God's Word is a lamp unto our feet, and a light unto our path (Psalms 119:105).

Prayerfully, this devotional will serve to shine light into any dark areas in our lives.

TABLE OF CONTENTS

DAY 1

Faith: Complete and consistent trust or confidence in God based on our relationship with Him...

And Jesus answering saith unto them, Have faith in God. For verily I say unto you, That whosoever shall say unto this mountain, Be thou removed, and be thou cast into the sea; and shall not doubt in his heart, but shall believe that those things which he saith shall come to pass; he shall have whatsoever he saith. (Mark 11:22-23)

IT IS BY OUR CONFESSION OF FAITH that we receive salvation. Once we make that confession, grace steps in and moves us from the kingdom of darkness into the kingdom of light. God gives us a measure of faith that becomes the foundation that we build our relationship with Him.   Trials and tribulations come to test our faith in God. The rain

1

and winds of life descend upon us to see how deeply rooted we are in Him.

Each situation we face is a learning opportunity to see God at work. Every struggle reveals the righteousness and faithfulness of God as we go from faith to faith. We go through a process where we grow in grace and a deeper knowledge of Jesus Christ. God places us in a trial to perform a faith check to determine the state of our roots and spiritual fruit.

In Mark 11, Jesus performs a faith check through the illustration of the fig tree. He knows that the disciples have left everything they have known to follow Him. They have heard His teachings, and they have witnessed them at work through the power of miracles. There are also people who continuously surround Him as He ministers. The time for Jesus to fulfill His purpose has drawn near. Now He wants to know where their faith is rooted.

What if Jesus asked you to do a faith check? Maybe you have been going through something for a long time. The roots of doubt, unbelief, worry or anxiety are causing your foundation to shift. You start to wonder if breakthrough is near. You have cried out to God daily, waiting for Him to incline His ear to you and deliver you out of your afflictions. The mountain hasn't moved as quickly as you wanted.

Sometimes faith is the hardest thing for us to exercise unless we see immediate results. When we begin a workout regimen, our muscles respond to being stretched and contracted in strenuous exercises. We experience pain because we haven't worked our bodies at this higher level of activity before. We know that with no pain, there is no gain.

Paul gives us an illustration of an athlete running a race for a prize in 1 Corinthians 9:24-27. As a servant of God, his prize is an incorruptible crown. Paul must train his body to submit to the will of the Lord as he endures each trial. If he doesn't exercise his faith and show self-control, Paul risks being disqualified to preach to others. He loses his witness of his faith. When we walk by faith, we are showing people around us that we believe God. We trust His word. If He said it, that settles it. No matter what it looks like, we must have faith that His word will not return void. He watches over His word to perform it.

Noah can testify to what it means to trust God. In Genesis 6:8-22, He receives a word from the Lord to build an ark because of a future flood as punishment for unrepentant sin. It has never rained before, but Noah still obeys God. We can only imagine the ridicule as people probably begin to question whether he really heard from God. Noah has complete trust in Him. In God's timing, the rains fall from the sky. Noah witnesses the manifestation of God's word. God makes a covenant with Noah because of his steadfastness to abound in the work of the Lord. He aligned his faith with God's will for his life.

What are you believing God to do in your life? Have you allowed other voices or your emotions to shake the foundation of your faith? In whom or what have you placed your trust? Faith is so important in our walk with God. We can move the mountains in our lives if we do not doubt. Just remember that whatever we ask for must line up with God's will.

Ephesians 2:8, Hebrews 11:6, Hebrews 12:1-2

ᴿᴹ MY REFLECTIONS ᴹᴿ

_____

_____

_____

_____

_____

_____

_____

_____

_____

_____

_____

_____

_____

_____

DAY 2

Submission to God: The daily process of yielding to God's will and living our lives as a spiritual sacrifice to Him...

Submit yourselves therefore to God. Resist the devil, and he will flee from you. (James 4:7)

TODDLERS DO NOT LIKE TO SURRENDER TO SLEEP. They run around, throw tantrums or devise crafty ways to delay what their body needs most. When toddlers grow into teenagers, the battle for control does not end. Teens discover they have a mind and a will, and they are not afraid to start showing it to their parents or guardians. Time and experience teach children that their parents are only trying to protect them and lead them on the right path.

As children of God, we struggle with surrendering to Him. It is not an easy thing to do because we give up control of what we know and want. From the world's perspective, surrendering is a sign of weakness. It means someone or something is taking away our freedom and independence or our right to choose. We can't pursue what pleases us.

Adam was in total submission when God first created him. He worked the garden as God's steward, managing it according to His will. God allowed him to name all the animals and presented him with a help meet to end his loneliness. Adam's wife submitted to him in the same manner that he surrendered to God (Genesis 2:20-24; 1 Peter 3:1-7). Even though Adam committed himself to God, the enemy of this world deceived his mind into thinking that the creation knew more than the Creator. Not submitting to God led Adam down the wrong path.

When we become believers in Christ, we realize that we are in the world and not of the world. Our minds are no longer conformed to the ways of this life. God renews our mind so that we can show His good, acceptable and perfect will. Surrendering to God is returning the product back over to the Maker for finetuning and maintenance.

Since God is our travel guide and we don't know the route, wouldn't it be easier for us to follow as He leads? He is omniscient. He foresees the pitfalls, escape routes and snares where the snakes and wolves congregate (Isaiah 35:7-10). The devil is roaring like a lion ready to devour us and steal our spiritual destiny like Adam.

Submitting to God protects us from detours and delays like the prodigal son endured in Luke 15:11-18. The prodigal son wanted his inheritance before he was ready to handle the accountability assigned to it. Like the teenagers mentioned earlier, he wanted to exert his mind and will over his father's. He lost it all and endured lack while forced to work in a pigpen. The father extended grace when the prodigal son submitted to him. Surrendering to God means walking away from our plans and giving Him our "yes."

Mary, the mother of Jesus, surrendered her plans to marry Joseph and have children when they desired in Luke 1:38. She risked losing her fiancé and damaging her reputation to submit to God. Her love for Him was greater than the approval of the world. God blessed her obedience with an overflow of blessings and honor. Our personal plans and aspirations should be secondary to God's plan, word, and will for our lives. When we seek His kingdom and righteousness first, everything else will be added to us according to His will and timing (Matthew 6:33).

Jesus is our true example of total submission to the will of God. In Philippians 2:5-8, Jesus humbled Himself to become obedient to death. He came down from His throne to become the propitiation for our sins. He sacrificed His will for the will of the one who sent Him. The devil tempted Him with every desire of this world, but Jesus surrendered to His purpose. In the Garden of Gethsemane, the weight of what He had to do burdened Him until He sweated drops of blood. In the end, He still submitted to God and became the Way, the Truth and the Life to our salvation. Where would we be if He had not given God His "yes?"

What areas of your life do you need to surrender completely to God?

1 Peter 3:15, Luke 9:23, Psalm 143:10

↤ MY REFLECTIONS ↦

_____

_____

_____

_____

_____

_____

_____

_____

_____

_____

_____

_____

DAY 3

Prayer: Two-way communication with God that involves asking, praising and listening...

And he spake a parable unto them to this end, that men ought always to pray, and not to faint; (Luke 18:1)

IMAGINE A GRASSY PATHWAY that leads through an opening surrounded by palm trees. Behind the trees is a large pond. A wooden bridge crosses over a section of the water and connects to the other side. Birds fly overhead. Every now and then, they skip across the water or perch gracefully on the ground. The sun beams brightly in one spot while the ocean breeze wraps around the trees like a comforting blanket. It is a place of peace, rest and intimacy. It is inviting and secluded. We can sit on that wooden bridge for a spell, release our cares and meditate on things that are pure, lovely, praiseworthy and of a good report.

We have access to a spiritual place like this 24 hour a day. We call it the practice of prayer.

Prayer is the privilege to come to God in an intimate way. We express our love and devotion to God, and that expression shows our dependence on Him. With expectation and hope, we can ask and receive, seek and find and knock and open doors. Because of our connection to Him, we can have access to all things that pertain to life and godliness. Jesus prayed many times throughout the day. His disciples became so intrigued that they asked Him to teach prayer to them. He knew that His dependence on God strengthened Him to handle situations and make wise decisions regarding ministry.

Prayer is a place with God where we're not judged. We can be vulnerable with the Lord. In Psalms 139, David tells us that there is nowhere we can go from His Spirit. He knows our uprising and down sitting. Before we were bones knitting together in a fetal frame, God knew us and had a plan for us. Prayer keeps us grounded in who God is and what His word says. It provides a place where He becomes our strong tower and we can run inside and feel safe. We can confess our sins, failures and insecurities, and God is faithful to forgive, redirect and surround us with His grace, love and mercy.

Prayer is our own personal road map for our lives. We seek direction and repentance, intercede for others, and thank God for His goodness. Nehemiah was a man of intercession. When his kinsmen told him about the state of Jerusalem, he immediately prayed to God. Nehemiah repented, and God gave him a strategy for rebuilding the city. With every step, there was opposition. He could have listened to or consulted with those around him, but Nehemiah remained in prayer and continued with his purpose. When the building was complete, Nehemiah led the people into praise, worship and prayer to honor God for what He had done.

How often do we seek God for a plan or His decision? Do we make the decision first and then ask God to make it happen? If He truly directs our paths, He should be the source of our lives and not a resource we approach for our own purposes.

Prayer is a place where Hannah's deepest desires were answered even though she was misunderstood by man. Hannah's barrenness caused her much sorrow. Her husband's second wife taunted her constantly. Even though her husband favored her, Hannah desperately wanted a child, and she prayed year after year in the temple. In 1 Samuel 1:26-27, Hannah rejoiced in her answered prayer and dedicated her child, Samuel, to the Lord.

Prayer is a time to be silent and listen to God speak. How many times do we pray to God about what's on our hearts, but we never ask what's on His heart? We sometimes enter prayer with our own agenda and seek God to provide solutions to our problems. There is nothing wrong with making our petitions to God.

We must realize that it is not a one-way communication. God wants to share His agenda with us.

Ask the Lord what's on His heart today. What is one way that you can improve your prayer life?

Psalm 139:4, Jeremiah 33:3, Hebrews 4:16

⟪ᴍᴡ MY REFLECTIONS ᴍᴡ⟫

_____

_____

_____

_____

_____

_____

_____

_____

_____

_____

_____

_____

_____

DAY 4

Spiritual Discipline: Practices that promote spiritual growth, such as studying God's word, changing mindsets and living a God-first life...

Know ye not, that to whom ye yield yourselves servants to obey, his servants ye are to whom ye obey. (Romans 6:16)

IF WE ARE TO COMPETE IN A RACE, we must be physically fit. Therefore, we must be spiritually fit to compete in the race that is set before us and lay aside every weight. If we want to lose weight for health or personal reasons, we must adhere to a diet that will produce the desired results. Therefore, we must be careful what we feed our spirits.

Thoughts and emotions can hinder us. They are flesh-based instead of Word-based. Anything carnal puts us at enmity with God. We are supposed to carry the weight of God's glory, not the weight of our afflictions. Paul says in 2 Corinthians 4:17-18 that the affliction is light and temporary. If we do not engage in spiritual practices that keep our minds stayed on Him, we push back the affliction's expiration date.

When we don't allow the Holy Spirit to come in fully and enlighten our spiritual eyes through daily fellowship, those besetting sins become strongholds. Strongholds eventually become cycles. Spiritual discipline is necessary to walking successfully with Christ and being delivered from the bondage of sin.

How much of our day is truly dedicated to God? Not just listening to gospel songs on our way to work or checking in weekly to church. Are we continually seeking God throughout our whole day?

Some people start their morning with a cup of coffee and plan out their work day. Some may focus on the bills they have to pay or the struggles their children face. Some may question which medication to take or why they must wake up this early.

Others greet God with a "Good morning" and lie prostrate before Him in worship. Others pray and make declarations about their day or read the Bible. How do you start your day?

On the day of Pentecost, the disciples gathered in one room on one accord to be filled with the Holy Spirit. The Holy Spirit manifested through the speaking of tongues and preaching. This divine demonstration led to 3,000 people being saved. In Acts 2:42 the apostles made spiritual discipline a daily part of their lives. In fact, Acts 6:1-5 tells us that the apostles appointed people to serve the followers because they needed time to stay in sync with the Holy Spirit. Their spiritual discipline prepared them to minister, perform miracles and handle religious opposition.

If we scheduled time in our day for spiritual discipline, would we have more peace for the day's events? Maybe we can't receive all our daily bread and benefits (Matthew 6:11; Psalms 68:19) because we don't practice spiritual discipline. We must break spiritual bread with God before we break bread with our families. Remember Moses and Jesus said that we don't live by bread alone, but by every word that comes out of God's mouth (Deuteronomy 8:3; Matthew 4:4). These men were both in the wilderness and experienced trials and temptations. They knew that God was all they needed. Are you in a wilderness situation now? Is life throwing things at you from all directions?

Maybe it is time to sit at the Master's feet and let Him change your focus and mindset.

That was what Mary did in Luke 10:38-42. While Martha complained about serving, Mary found refuge in serving Jesus by seeking that one thing: His presence. Her yielding was in obedience to Him.

To grow as believers, we must practice spiritual discipline. Our calling depends on it.

Romans 5:3-5, 2 Peter 1:10,
2 Thessalonians 1:11-12

⟨ᴍ MY REFLECTIONS ᴍ⟩

DAY 5

Obedience: being a doer of God's word...

If you love me, keep my commandments. (John 14:15)

THE WORD OF GOD MAKES IT CLEAR that we are to obey Him every time. We forfeit blessings when we do not follow His commandments (Deuteronomy 28:1:13; Leviticus 26:1-13). We often declare that we are blessed when we come and when we go. We are the head, and not the tail; we are the lender, and not the borrower. Let's return to Deuteronomy 28:1, shall we? The word of the Lord states that we must hearken diligently to His voice and observe to do all His commandments. Then we receive the blessings.

We are to obey those who have rule over us. On our jobs, in our marriages, in our churches and yes, in our government, we are to submit to authority (Romans

21

13:1-8). Our flesh will not automatically do this because of our sin nature and self-will.

As the poet Emily Dickinson wrote, "The heart wants what it wants – or else it does not care." Our flesh wants our way in our timing. We must submit our flesh to the unction of the Holy Spirit to walk in obedience.

Our children should also obey us like we obey our Father in heaven. We must teach our children obedience, so they will be law-abiding citizens. Remember all authority is of God and when we are out of order, disobedience is the result. Punishment follows disobedience, and disobedience brings about curses (Deuteronomy 28:15-25; Leviticus 26:14-25).

We are quick to discipline our children for disobedience, but is it something we're lacking ourselves? Can we assure our children that we practice what we preach? Or do we replicate King Saul?

King Saul could not obey simple commandments from God, and it cost him the Kingdom (1 Samuel 13:13-14). Saul allowed flesh to cause him to disobey. God had already given him the victory once over Israel's enemy, the Philistines. As with all spiritual warfare, the enemy returned for another attack. Saul should have had confidence in God to give him the victory again. He wanted to test Saul's obedience. God delayed Samuel's coming. Everyone abandoned Saul. The Philistines tightened their garrison around him. Saul's flesh got the best of him.

His fear of man overruled his fear of God.

Obedience involves more than just keeping His commandments. God wants to know if we will obey when He doesn't come according to our timetable. The issue wasn't Saul's sacrifice; it was his obedience (1 Samuel 15:22).

When we are partially obedient, we are still in total disobedience. In Acts 5:1-10, Ananias and Sapphira sold their possessions. They kept part of the money and gave the rest to Peter. This act was complete disobedience. Ananias and Sapphira presented their offering as if it were the whole amount. Their dishonesty led to their destruction.

Not obeying God is rebellion. Being stubborn in our ways and disregarding God's commands are sins that hurt His heart. God the Father, the Son and the Holy Spirit want to make their abode in us through our obedience (John 14:23), but they can't if rebellion which is witchcraft and stubbornness which is idolatry live in our hearts (1 Samuel 15:23). We want to be filled and flooded with His presence. We can't let our fleshly desires get in the way.

What areas of your life are you being totally or partially obedient? What haven't you done yet? Maybe you did it your way instead of God's way. Do you love Him? Then always obey Him.

Psalm 128:1-2, Psalm 51:16-17, Luke 17:6-10

ᚼᚼ MY REFLECTIONS ᚼᚼ

DAY 6

***Wisdom: Divine, practical knowledge
and insight that guides our daily lives...***

---

*Now if any of you lack wisdom, let him ask of
God, that giveth to all men liberally, and
upbraideth not; and it shall be given to him.
(James 1:5)*

FOR THE BELIEVER OUR CHOICES AND
DECISIONS are made with God's purposes and
desires in mind. We look to God to instruct us where
we should go. When Isaac faced a famine in Gerar,
God told him to avoid going to Egypt and remain
where he was (Genesis 26:1-6). This direction
doesn't make sense in the natural. There were no
resources around to sustain him. Isaac learned
through experience about the character of God.

God is the source of all things; His wisdom and knowledge are deep, and His ways are past finding out (Romans 11:33-36).

God's word of wisdom gave Isaac a strategy to open places that others deemed permanently closed. The foolishness of God was wiser than men (1 Corinthians 1:25). As Isaac dug into each well, water always flowed with abundance. Isaac's enemies made a covenant with him because they saw the glory of God.

Wisdom can give us a divine strategy, plan, creative idea or solution to help us during a physical, financial or spiritual famine. We must ask God to tell us what to do, how to do it and when to do it. Has God ever asked us to make a move in a direction that doesn't make logical sense? We tend to value our intellect over divine knowledge.

Instead of trying to figure it out, be wise and let God work it out.

Wisdom flows from a reverence for God. It is the process of discernment that keeps us from bad choices and wicked people (Proverbs 27:9). Sometimes bad choices are decisions we make with good intention instead of God intention. In 1 Chronicles 13:7-10 David's servant, Uzzah assisted with transporting the ark of God from the house of Abinadab. With a good motive, he attempted to prevent the ark from falling over to the ground. He reverenced the presence of God. It was a bad choice because he went against God's command.

Wisdom helps us to wait on God and stop trying to help Him out.

God promised a child to Abram and Sarai. Time kept passing by. Doubt and discouragement crept into Sarai's mind. She decided to help God out and asked Abram to sleep with her maid (Genesis 16:2-4). She lacked wisdom in this decision. Her plan led to family strife, jealousy and bitterness. It didn't bind up the wounds of her heart.

God's plans are whole and perfect. His wisdom turns our weeping into joy. Even though they did not seek God's wisdom, He still gave them His promise---Isaac. And Sarai laughed at the awesomeness of God (Genesis 21:1-6).

God is liberal in giving wisdom. In 1 Kings 3:5-15, King Solomon requested wisdom from God. God gave it to him liberally. He desired a spiritual gift. If God gave us the opportunity to ask for anything, would we request material or spiritual gifts?

I Kings 3:16-27 exemplifies the use of wisdom in our lives today. Solomon sought the Lord and did not lean to his own understanding. He knew how to govern God's people. His gift of wisdom spared a child's life. The use of godly wisdom will spare us great grief and mistakes.

Whose wisdom have you been seeking lately: man's or God's?

Ephesians 5:15-17, Proverbs 8:33-36,
Proverbs 9:10-11

ᨆ MY REFLECTIONS ᨆ

_____

_____

_____

_____

_____

_____

_____

_____

_____

_____

_____

_____

_____

_____

_____

_____

DAY 7

Integrity: Honest character and upright nature that is whole and undivided in moral principles; an inside job...

The just man walketh in his integrity: his children are blessed after him. (Proverbs 20:7)

WATER IS PURE IN ITS NATURAL state. It is transparent and free from contaminants. The purity of water allows it to flow through all living things and provide nourishment. Dirt, oil and other pollutants can seep into the water. Their presence prevents water from fulfilling its purpose. When outside elements permeate the integrity of the water and impede its flow, the whole earth and all that is in it suffer from thirst.

When we make decisions that do not align with God's word, we compromise the integrity of our vessels.

One wrong thought, ill-spoken word or unwise action has the power to contaminate the living water inside of us like a little leaven leavening the whole lump (Galatians 5:9; Mark 8:15). It can also destroy our witness as followers of Jesus Christ. We represent the kingdom of heaven. Our integrity should influence the world (Matthew 13:33).

What is the current state of our vessels? Have we compromised our integrity in any way?

We may immediately say that we have not because we think of integrity as doing the right thing even when no one is watching. If we are truthful with ourselves, we know that the omniscient God is ever present with eyes searching throughout the whole earth to show Himself strong in those with hearts perfect toward Him (2 Chronicles 16:9). He is a discerner of thoughts and motives, especially ones motivated by false humility or flesh.

We may also think of integrity as having a good name among people in our fields of influence, such as our families, co-workers, churches or communities. Although a good name is better than riches (Proverbs 22:1), integrity has everything to do with the choices we make and very little to do with our reputations. It is more important to the Lord than sacrifice because having an honest character is being obedient to God's commands.

We are given a measure of faith, but we are held accountable for a measure of integrity grounded in His will. Not only is the world watching and listening, but our household knows if we are saying one thing and living another. How we live teaches our children and grandchildren how to be morally upright. What we do determines if we release generational blessings or curses. Our integrity really does matter.

When we do not walk in His integrity, we do not bear the reflection of the Lord (Proverbs 27:19; 2 Corinthians 3:18). He is a God of truth, holiness and righteousness. We dishonor Him when we do not live according to our true kingdom identity. We are called to be a chosen generation, a holy nation and a royal priesthood set apart for His glory (1 Peter 2:9).

The disciple John tells us about the man who laid at the pool of Bethesda (John 5:1-14). John says in verse 6 that "when Jesus saw him *lie* [emphasis added] and knew that he had been now a long time in that case, he saith unto him, "Wilt thou be made whole?" Jesus saw his physical position and spiritual condition. The impotent man was not living true to his kingdom identity. His continuous cycle of depending on man for deliverance blocked him from seeing the Word as his present help!

Job and Joseph are two examples of just men who walked in integrity. Job remained whole and undivided in his moral convictions as he underwent great loss and suffering (Job 2:3, 9; Job 27:5), while Joseph maintained his integrity when Potiphar's wife tried to force him to sleep with her (Genesis 39:7-12). God honored their integrity through restoration, prosperity and promotion.

How will you walk in His integrity daily?

Proverbs 11:3, Proverbs 21:3, 1 Peter 2:13-17

ᗯᗯ *MY REFLECTIONS* ᗯᗯ

_____

_____

_____

_____

_____

_____

_____

_____

_____

_____

_____

_____

_____

_____

_____

_____

DAY 8

Purity: Freedom from immorality,
especially of a sexual nature;
consecration of one's body unto the
Lord...

If a man therefore purge himself from these,
he shall be a vessel unto honor, sanctified and
meet for the master's use and prepared unto
every good work. (2 Timothy 2:21)

THE BEATITUDES ARE SOME of the most familiar verses to believers. They illustrate examples of what a blessed life is. In Matthew 5:8, Jesus says that those who have a pure heart will see God. What does a pure heart look like? Are we born with it? Does it always stay pure?

If we really examine Matthew 5-7, we realize that purity is a common thread. To be light and salt, we must be pure and our bodies devoid of darkness. Fasting, giving and praying must be done to honor the Father and not ourselves. Our priorities must be heavenly focused, and our hearts must be set on loving and blessing our enemies. We judge the quality of our own lives instead of judging others. Purity is allowing God's word to wash us daily and make us a holy and unblemished church unto God (Ephesians 5:26-27).

A pure heart calls out the Lord's name, prophesies, cast out devils and does great works according to His will so it can be kingdom bound (Matthew 7:21-23). It feeds the hungry, clothes the physically and spiritually naked with love and ministers to the sick and imprisoned (Matthew 25:40-45). A pure heart hides God's word so that it might not sin against Him (Psalm 119:11). It is having a heart like Jesus and enabling people to see the God in us.

Enoch was a man who walked upright before the Lord. His heart must have been pure because he was translated to heaven without even experiencing death. The Lord saw Himself in Enoch and wanted him to come home. Are our hearts pure enough right now to be translated to heaven? Would God be able to see His reflection in us?

Purity means loving God with our whole heart and having a mindset that satisfies His will. David asked God to create in him a clean heart and renew a right spirit within him (Psalm 51:10). Purity is having a heart free from hatred, jealousy, lust and all works of the flesh. We must mortify these deeds and put to death our sinful habits through the power of the Holy Ghost (Galatians 5:17-21; Colossians 3:5-10).

Anything that detracts from the purity God desires is perversion. When we manipulate scripture to justify our actions or to please the world, we are not operating in purity. Balaam is a prime example. He perverted the gift of prophecy for material gain, but the Lord would not let him prophesy curses over His people. If we add or take away from God's word, we will be held accountable (Deuteronomy 12:32, Proverbs 30:6, Revelations 22:18).

Lust is an enemy to our purity and a gateway to perversion. Paul tells us in 1 Corinthians 6:15-20 that we were bought with a price to be a temple for the Holy Spirit. We cannot fall victim to the internal war going on inside of us. We must put off the former conversation that yields to deceitful lust and put on the new man created in righteousness and true holiness (Ephesians 4:22-24).

Feeding the flesh starves the spirit, reaps corruption and kills purpose. Just ask Samson. He lost his 1st wife to an enemy attack. He satisfied his flesh through fornication with a harlot, but his lust for Delilah, a Philistine woman, caused his downfall (Judges16:5-20). From birth he was set apart to live a holy life and be a warrior for God. He developed a soul tie to a woman who did not truly honor the things of God. Being unequally yoked robbed him of his vision and strength. He lost the presence of God; the people lost a judge whom God entrusted to protect them.

Lust begins in the mind. If we entertain the thought long enough, we are subject to manifest our thinking into sinful action that separates us from God. Even if we don't act upon it, have we still sinned (Matthew 5:27-28)? Are your thoughts and actions preparing your spiritual womb to birth or abort purpose? Let us not be ignorant of the enemy's devices.

1 Corinthians 7:32-35, Psalms 27:2-4, John 17:17-23

ᑫᔰ MY REFLECTIONS ᔬᒼ

_____

_____

_____

_____

_____

_____

_____

_____

_____

_____

_____

_____

DAY 9

Singleness: The quality or state of being single, unmarried or separate from others.

I say therefore to the unmarried and widows, it is good for them if they abide even as I. (1 Corinthians 7:8)

A REHEARSAL IS DEFINED BY ONLINE DICTIONARIES as private practice for a future public performance. Children practice speeches for holiday programs. Actors rehearse their lines for theatrical performances. Musicians go through multiple sets before a concert. Any time a person gets in front of an audience or even a class or boardroom meeting, he or she has to practice what to say or do. This practice allows the final act to flow naturally and seamlessly as if it is second nature. A rehearsal is an act of preparation.

41

Singleness is also a rehearsal for marriage. It is making ourselves whole and ready for our God-selected mates. During this process, the Lord deals with us in His own special way. It is an undetermined stretch of time where God takes His time to bring us the right person at the right time. In 2 Corinthians 6:14-18, Paul tells us that we cannot be unequally yoked. We may think that we know what is best for us, but we must trust the process.

If we look at the suffix –ness in the word singleness, we would see that it is defined as to render, simplify, beautify or to become. When we are single, we are on the potter's wheel as in Jeremiah 18:1-6. There is a time and season for all things as promised in Ecclesiastes 3:1-11, and it is in these times of singleness that God is using every experience as an opportunity for the single person to grow closer to Him and grow in their personal faith and devotion.

Singleness allows our hearts to be open to hear from the Lord so we can ask for the right things because we have the right priorities like Solomon (Song of Solomon 5:2; 1 Kings 3:5). When we focus on godliness, we become beautiful lights that attract greatness. The queen of Sheba heard about King Solomon's fame. The people around her talked that talk so good that she assembled a caravan to find out for herself if it were all true (1 Kings 10: 1-10). She wasn't only impressed with his riches, position, wisdom or servants. To be honest, the queen already possessed that; she was a complete woman financially, intellectually, emotionally and so on. The queen of Sheba had no more spirit in her when she noticed his ascent into the house of the Lord. His worship demonstrated how he treated people he loved. If he had that type of relationship with God, how much more would he treat his mate? The queen of Sheba gave King Solomon an abundance of gifts that helped his purpose: building God's temple. Singleness enables us to have vision to seek someone who will not distract us from the things of God.

Being single is more accepted today than in the past. Some men and women never marry by choice; it does not mean they're lonely. They have more time and opportunity to devote to the Lord in kingdom work and develop a deeper relationship with Him.

Timothy was a single young man devoted to the work of the Lord. Paul encouraged him to flee fornication and youthful lusts which can only be controlled through the power of the Holy Spirit (1 Timothy 4:1-8). Some lusts may include pride, arrogance, power and money, not just sexual temptation. Paul's lifestyle and letters to his spiritual son, Timothy, gave him a roadmap on how to live as a man of God.

Being singled out is not a negative; it is quite positive. We're separated because there is a special gift inside of us that must be developed for greater glory and purpose. Esther goes through a purification process to prepare her as a potential wife for King Ahasuerus (Esther 2:8-17). Her marriage had a greater purpose, for God called her to the kingdom for such a time as this to be a deliverer of a nation (Esther 4: 14-17). Even John the Baptist was separated relationally and socially to bring reformation and initiate the eternal dress rehearsal for God's bride (John 3:26-27). We must become a bride of the Master before we can become a bride of man. Singleness, whether relational, social or spiritual, is preparation for submission to something bigger. What greater purpose are you being separated for?

Psalm 62:5-8, 1 Corinthians 12:9-10, 1 Thessalonians 4:3-7

ᕯᘚ *MY REFLECTIONS* ᘚᕯ

_____

_____

_____

_____

_____

_____

_____

_____

_____

_____

_____

_____

DAY 10

***Marriage: A union between man and
woman who are in covenant with God...***

---

*Husbands, love your wives, even as Christ also
loved the church, and gave himself for it.
(Ephesians 5:25)*

MEN AND WOMEN ARE AS DIFFERENT as night
and day, but we're created by God to complement
one another. Marriage is a union ordained by God
between a man and a woman according to Genesis
2:21-25. Men and women were created in the image
of God with physical and emotional needs that only
another human being could meet. Marriage is meant
to be strong, exclusive and monogamous. Men and
women become one flesh that has an order. In 1
Corinthians 11:3, that order is God, Jesus, husband
and wife.

Because the wife is listed last doesn't mean she is of lesser or no importance. In Proverbs 31:1-31, Solomon extols the true worth of a wife. For she is a virtuous woman who is more than rubies, and God entrusts her with her husband's heart (verses 10-11). In fact, Proverbs 18:22 states that it is a good thing for a man to find a wife because he gains God's favor. God's favor is a shield that blesses us continually. No, the husband is listed before the wife because he is protecting his most precious thing: his wife (Ephesians 5:28-33). God does the same thing with His bride, Israel. In Ezekiel 16:8-14, He spreads His skirt over her to protect her virtue and adorns her with the most beautiful jewels. In fact, John tells us in Revelation 19:7-9 that there will be a supper for the Bridegroom and His bride, and she will be dressed in garments of righteousness.

Marriage is a pattern in the earth that reflects the reality of heaven. The order is divine, not inferior. It does not include the world's construction or deconstruction of the marital institution. We really have to ask ourselves some serious questions: What are our actions teaching the next generation about marriage? Will they see the scriptures fulfilled in our marriages, or are we conformed to the world's system? *Have we let dead flies get into our oil so that we are not prepared to meet the Bridegroom when He returns* (Ecclesiastes 10:1; Matthew 25:6-13)?

Husbands are the covering for their wives. They have a priestly role as intercessor, leader and protector of their families (Luke 11:21-22). A husband fathers the nations, while his wife births them. It is a mutual relationship of honor, respect, submission, and most importantly, love. Marriage is a mirror image of the individual relationship husband and wife have with God. Husbands and wives are one flesh that work together unto the purposes of God.

When we allow other doctrines, other people's opinions or outside connections to infiltrate our relationship with our spouses or God, we commit adultery and work against those purposes. God used the prophet Hosea's marriage (Hosea 1-3) as a real-life parable to illustrate how Israel had defiled their covenant with God. In Hosea 10:1&12, God requires the people of Israel to break up the fallow ground of their hearts because they are producing fruit of the flesh and not of the Spirit.

Our government always gives a State of the Union address to let us know how we are doing as a nation. Perhaps we need to do a state of the union address with our spouses and God. Let's look at the book of Ezekiel again. God used this prophet to see firsthand the state of Israel's spiritual union with Him. The spirit of the Lord carried Ezekiel to a valley of dry bones in chapter 37. Those bones were strewn around, broken apart and disconnected. They suffered from a lack of spiritual water that only comes from the word and Spirit of God. God asked Ezekiel a simple question: Son of man, can these bones live (verse 3)?

For them to live again, God had to cause His breath to enter. A marriage is only as strong as its structure, and structure comes from a sound order founded in God. His word orders our steps, marriages and covenant with God. That structure cannot stand if the heart is made of stone instead of flesh (Ezekiel 36:24-28).

So, what is the state of your unions? Allow the Lord to give you a new perspective. Your marriage to your spouse or God is not dead; it is only sleeping waiting for its resurrection.

Proverbs 5:15-21, Proverbs 31:10-11, 1 Corinthians 7:1-5, 1 Peter 3:1-8

ᕙ MY REFLECTIONS ᕗ

_____

_____

_____

_____

_____

_____

_____

_____

_____

_____

_____

DAY 11

Love: A fruit of the Holy Spirit that demonstrates unselfish, unconditional concern and strong affection for others; God's merciful nature towards His children...

For God so loved the world, that he gave his only begotten Son, that whosoever believeth in him should not perish, but have everlasting life. (John 3:16)

THERE WAS A WOMAN who loved to create with her hands. One day she walked through Target and saw a pottery wheel toy set. The little girl in her rejoiced. She took the set home. Her fingers moistened the clay with water and kneaded it into different creations. Suddenly, a new shape emerged: first, a head, next a torso, and then facial features. She cradled the figure in her hands like a treasured child.

Then the woman wept like Jesus when He felt compassion for His creation. The Holy Spirit whispered into her ear, "Come, let us make man in our image." He gave her a revelation of the love the Creator had for His creation. Do we really have a true revelation of God's love?

Love is a supernatural force that is naturally misunderstood.

We try to define it according to our terms. We humanize a heavenly attribute that can only be experienced. We must realize that love is the most powerful and motivating expression of God. It is an intricate part of His character.

Despite what some may think, love is not a feeling that comes and goes. It is not a piece of clothing that we can discard when it no longer fits into our vision. Love is the more excellent way, a type of grace that thrives on connection.

Ruth had this type of love for Naomi. She was a Moabite who had married Naomi's son. When Naomi lost her husband and children, she told Ruth and Orpah that they could return to their homes. Orpah left immediately as she wept over the loss of her husband and now her mother-in-law. However, Ruth would not abandon her. She had witnessed firsthand God's devotion, love and faithfulness.

Ruth made a declaration, "Entreat me not to leave thee, or to return from following after thee: for whither thou goest, I will go; and where thou lodgest,

I will lodge: thy people shall be my people, and thy God my God: Where thou diest, will I die, and there will I be buried: the LORD do so to me, and more also, if ought but death part thee and me (Ruth 1:16-17)."

She put aside selfish interests for someone who needed compassion, companionship and grace. Ruth eventually married Boaz and gave birth to Obed, a forefather to David and a descendant in the royal bloodline of Jesus (Ruth 4:13-17). Her unselfish act of love was a precursor to what Jesus would do for us. How many unselfish acts have we done today, last week, last month or last year? Are we really sacrificing for love?

Love challenges us to put into practice the works of Christ by loving our enemies, overlooking offenses and fulfilling God's law. It is a divine call to forgive, witness and give with no limitations. Showing agape love is a powerful, evangelistic tool that can cause sinners to be saved, broken families to be healed and hearts to be mended. God's love for mankind is the same kind that the father had for his prodigal son; it was unconditional. The son erred in his judgment, but his father was willing to forgive and take him back without making him feel guilty (Luke 15:11-32).

We view love as a gift that we can take back when we are hurt. Jesus had every right to stop loving Peter because of his denial. In John 21:15-17, Jesus reminds Peter that if he loved Him, Peter must feed His sheep. Have you only been feeding His sheep who are already in the fold? Have you forgotten the lost ones?

Romans 5:8, 1 Corinthians 13:4-8,
1 John 4:16-17

⟪∿ MY REFLECTIONS ∿⟫

_____

_____

_____

_____

_____

_____

_____

_____

_____

_____

_____

_____

_____

_____

_____

_____

DAY 12

Faithfulness: A fruit of the Holy Spirit that demonstrates unwavering loyalty, dedication and devotion; God's steadfast character of never leaving or forsaking His children...

Let us hold fast the profession of our faith without wavering; (for he is faithful that promised;) (Hebrews 10:23)

WILL YOU REMAIN LOYAL when the Lord allows the enemy to throw you into a fire seven times hotter because you refused to stop worshipping Him like Meshach, Shadrach and Abednego?

Will you continue to dedicate your life to serving Him when the people put you in prison and persecute you for speaking the truth like Jeremiah, Peter or Paul?

Will you unashamedly evangelize Abba's love to unbelievers who scorn you for your past mistakes like Mary Magdalene, the Samarian woman at the well or the woman caught in adultery?

The furnace of affliction tests the validity of our faithfulness to God.

If we are honest with ourselves, we would admit that there have been times when what we've endured made us question His faithfulness. We have read, prayed and declared the word, but our prayers remain unanswered. God produced an overflow that was more than we could ask or think, but at our most vulnerable point of need we seem to be in a famine where loss is evident and God is nowhere to be found.

If we believe in a God that we have never seen, then shouldn't we believe that He is still working out our victory we have yet to see? An invisible God manifests invisible rewards when we stop basing our breakthroughs on the visible.

Wavering faith leads to questions. Questions seduce us away from God's word and traps us inside our human reason. God may remain silent and allow the process to run its course, or He may also pose some questions to us just like he did Job in chapter 38. God asks Job who or what darkened his counsel because human reason was blocking the entrance of God's light. He was the God of creation who provided prey for the ravens so that their crying young lacked nothing (v. 41) and blessed Job with everything he lost (Job 29). Could He not restore?

Did Job really believe that God is the same yesterday, today and forevermore? Do you?

Was he just trying to appear righteous among his friends when he said that he could decree a thing and it would be established (Job 22:23)? Maybe the furnace of affliction comes to expose our own self-righteousness so that the fruit of faithfulness can abound.

The Lord does not change; we do (Malachi 3:6).

Faithfulness is an attribute of God. He is true to His character by unwavering in His promises and abounding in His love. In Hebrews 6:13-18, God says that He can swear by Himself because of His immutable character. In Lamentations 3:22-23, He is ever faithful because of the new mercies we see every morning. Even when we are disobedient or unforgiving, He is faithful and merciful. We made it to today because of His faithfulness. Shouldn't we believe that He is faithful to bring us through every future problem? Nothing is new under the sun to God.

The spirit of offense is an enemy to our faithfulness to God. It can cause us to walk away from a ministry. We must remember God's loyalty is not determined on what we do or do not do. He is the judge of what is right or fair, not us. We must be encouraged to remain faithful even in the face of opposition and persecution. Believers will be rewarded with eternal life for faithfulness.

Let us be faithful in all our doings like our Heavenly Father.

Romans 5:15, 1 Corinthians 10:13, Revelations 2:10

ᚼᚱ MY REFLECTIONS ᚼᚱ

_____

_____

_____

_____

_____

_____

_____

_____

_____

_____

_____

_____

_____

_____

_____

_____

DAY 13

Perseverance: A fruit of the Holy Spirit that demonstrates persistence and patience in doing something despite difficulty or delay in achieving success; God's eternal commitment of longsuffering toward us...

And let us not be weary in well doing: for in due season we shall reap if we faint not. (Galatians 6:9)

AFTER SURVIVING A DUCK BOAT ACCIDENT resulting in the death of her three children, her husband, and five other relatives, Tia Coleman struggles to mend the broken pieces of her life. Prayers sustain her during this arduous journey of grief, suffering, healing and restoration.

People who have experienced financial setbacks, one after the other, still prepare their tithes as an offering of worship and love to God. They continue to go to work and strive toward the hopes of walking in abundance.

A crowd blocks a paralyzed man from getting inside of a house. His friends do not give up. Their goal is to get him to Jesus so he can be healed. This hindrance doesn't defeat them; it sparks innovation instead. They make a hole in the roof and lower him down on his bed. Their determination and faith lead to the paralyzed man's healing and forgiveness of sins (Mark 2:1-5).

In a letter to the church of Philadelphia, John writes about Jesus' commendation of the congregation's work of keeping His command to persevere in the face of temptation. He offers them an eternal reward for their act of overcoming the world. They will become a pillar in the temple of God and receive a new name (Revelations 3:7-12 AMP).

Daniel perseveres in prayer when he endures opposition from the satraps. His foes envy him because he is a man of faith who operates in excellence. They search for anything damaging they can use to destroy his character. Finding nothing, they deceive the king into passing a law about praying to other gods to trap Daniel. Prayer gets him into the lion's den, and prayer is what gets him out. God could have prevented him from being put in that situation, but He orchestrated the opportunity to develop Daniel's perseverance and to show God's sovereignty. When we persevere for God, promotion and prosperity come forth (Daniel 6: 1-28).

When we find ourselves in the lion's den, do we immediately pray for an easy escape? Do we become emboldened with faith or embittered toward God? We could be missing an opportunity for spiritual development.

In each example, there is a situation that presents an opportunity to run away and give up or stay and endure. We also discover that those difficulties can arise even when we walk in integrity and excellence like Daniel.

Perseverance is the spiritual discipline of staying focused and steadfast in achieving any goal regardless of suffering and persecution. Longsuffering and patience are listed as fruit of the Spirit, and perseverance is connected to them. If we look up the word *longsuffering*, it is defined as having or showing patience despite troubles, especially those caused by other people. That definition matches our definition of perseverance.

Our perseverance through life's challenges serves as an example to unbelievers and a pattern to the household of faith (1 Timothy 1:16). The woman who presented her case in front of a worldly, unjust judge in Luke 18:3-8 showed perseverance. Her persistence persuaded him to rule in her favor even though he did not have any reverence for God or man. Her refusal to give up was not by her might or strength, but by the empowerment of the Holy Spirit.

God perseveres in His mercy toward us to repair our covenant relationship with Him. In the midst of a mocking crowd, Jesus, beaten beyond recognition, struggled to carry a block of wood down a rocky road. Through betrayal, abandonment, rejection and extreme pain, Jesus remained on the cross even though He had the power to send a legion of angels to rescue Him. He stayed focused on His purpose: to die so we could live.

How can reading and praying God's word help you improve your ability to persevere?

2 Corinthians 4:8-9, 2 Timothy 3:10-14, 2 Peter 1: 5-8

⟨ʷ *MY REFLECTIONS* ʷ⟩

_____

_____

_____

_____

_____

_____

_____

_____

_____

DAY 14

Self-control: A fruit of the Holy Spirit that demonstrates the ability to control oneself in emotions and desires, especially in difficult situations; God's temperance in not giving us what we truly deserve...

Wherefore, my beloved brethren, let every man be swift to hear, slow to speak, slow to wrath. (James 1:19)

SELF-CONTROL DOESN'T JUST HAPPEN OVERNIGHT. It is a daily process that must be put into practice because our flesh is in a sin battle with our spirit man. We as Christians must be cool under pressure by showing restraint and exercising discretion. Discretion preserves us, guides our affairs and defers our anger (Proverbs 2:11; Psalm 112:5; Proverbs 19:11). No matter what the situation is, we should always maintain a calm disposition and moderate our thoughts, mouths and emotions.

The woman with the issue of blood (Luke 8: 43-48) is often taught as a story of chronic illness that leads to isolation, debt and an exercise of faith. There are many areas of our lives where we haven't practiced self-control, and now we are "bleeding" all over the place. One source of our bleeding is our tongues (James 3:5-10). Our conversation can be flesh-driven if we do not have self-control, and the effects can be one of life or death (Proverbs 18:21).

Nabal was a great man who had many possessions and a beautiful wife of understanding. He was given much but wasn't very faithful over it. His rude speech and nasty actions infected and affected everyone around him. His wife often served as a peacemaker and offered grace to mediate situations. David and his men lived in the wilderness where Nabal's men sheared sheep. He sent word to Nabal to show favor toward his men since they did not harm Nabal's shearers. Nabal responds indignantly, "Who is David? and who is the son of Jesse? there be many servants now a days that break away every man from his master. Shall I then take my bread, and my water, and my flesh that I have killed for my shearers, and give it unto men, whom I know not whence they be (1 Samuel 25:10-11)?"

His response angered David, and he didn't show restraint in his thoughts or actions. He drew his sword and led his men to kill Nabal. Abigail stepped in, and her act of submission and grace reminded

David of the call on his life. His lack of self-control would bring shame and dishonor to him if he pursued this act of retaliation. When Abigail informed Nabal of the effects of his words and lack of self-control, his heart hardened and ten days later God struck him dead (1 Samuel 25:36-38). We must discipline our mouths to speak words that please God.

Wisdom helps us to exercise self-control, especially when we want to act on our emotions. Many scholars have said that Peter may have been impulsive. His tendency to act and speak without restraint caused him trouble and rebuke while coming against the prophecy Jesus was sent to fulfill. (Matthew 16:21-23; Matthew 26:51-54). When we have no self-control, we have no rule over our spirits. We are a like a city with broken down walls and no defense (Proverbs 25:28). We toss to and from with every wind of doctrine and become susceptible to doublemindedness and deception. We can speak the truth in love and mature into the image of Christ (Ephesians 4:14-15).

To develop self-control, we need a divine pattern to follow. Older men and women can train younger men and women in the church (Titus 2:1-8), but the best teacher is a godly life as a living example. Is there someone who can mentor you in how to be sober-minded, sound, and self-controlled in every situation?

God's power is limitless and able to control any situation. God's temperance or self-control is the best pattern to follow. His love for us prevents Him from truly giving us what we deserve. One who has compassion toward the Lord will be troubled and in distress when we rebel against His will (Jeremiah 31:20; Lamentations 1:20). Their spirit will feel convicted. However, God exercises self-control and gives us endless opportunities to get back into right alignment with His will.

How can you align your mouth, mind and actions with God's word so that you can produce the fruit of self-control?

Proverbs 16:32, Romans 13:14,
2 Corinthians 5:14

ᐊᵂ *MY REFLECTIONS* ᵂᐅ

_____

_____

_____

_____

_____

_____

_____

_____

_____

_____

DAY 15

Forgiveness: A fruit of the Holy Spirit that demonstrates the willingness to pardon a hurtful act; God's forbearance of us that He expects us to reciprocate toward others...

Bear with each other and forgive one another if any of you has a grievance against someone. Forgive as the Lord forgave you. (Colossians 3:13, NIV)

FORGIVENESS IS A DIFFICULT ACT to do, but it is one that we must practice as believers. No matter the offense or hurtful act, we must release people from owing us anything. An apology may never come from their lips. They may move on with their lives as if nothing has ever happened or feel that they were justified in their actions; nevertheless, God requires us to let go of vengeance, resentment, hurt, bitterness and unforgiveness. He promises us that all things work together for the good of those who love Him and are called to His purpose (Romans 8:28).

As God is making it work together, we still must process our emotions and battle our flesh through life's situations. Let us think about the last time we had to forgive someone. Maybe the situation caused so much anguish that thoughts ran through our minds like these:

I can forgive, but I can't forget...It's just not fair, Lord. I am over here suffering, and he is just living his life like he's on top of the world. When is he going to get what's coming to him? When I struggled with cancer, the one I loved walked away. I can't forgive her...My mother told me that she wished I was never born. It hurts so much. Lord, how can I forgive her? My son stole from me several times to feed his addiction. I can't trust him again...My boss let me go after several years of service due to budget cuts. I dedicated so much of my time and effort...The officers were found not guilty of shooting my unarmed son. I am filled with so much bitterness. How can I let it go?

Each thought bears the pain and presence of disappointment, discouragement, defeat and discontentment. However, through the power of the Holy Spirit, we can pardon the offense, separate it from the person and continue to walk in love toward that person.

Those offenses and hurtful acts are sometimes fiery darts thrown by the enemy. The adversary uses them to cause division and confusion, derail purpose and blessing and bring upon death and destruction. If we really reflect on times that forgiveness was the hardest to do, we would probably notice that those times involved family or close friends. People whom we have allowed ourselves to trust and be vulnerable with are the ones who wound us the deepest.

Joseph's brothers had thrown him into a pit because he shared his dream. After their father's death, they fell before him, begged for mercy and asked to be his servants. Joseph was in a good position to treat them in the harshest manner. Famine had overtaken the land. The brothers had no way to provide for themselves. Joseph wept and said to them. "Fear not: for am I in the place of God? But as for you, ye thought evil against me; but God meant it unto good, to bring to pass, as it is I this day, to save much people alive (Genesis 50: 19-20)." Joseph saw that God allowed it to happen for a greater purpose that later unfolds in the book of Exodus. He chose to forgive instead of meting out his own form of justice.

What if God meted out His justice instead of forgiving us? What if He held grudges like us and didn't send Jesus?

God's forgiveness removes our sins and restores our fellowship with Him, and it is always available (1 John 1:9). We must truly be sorry for our sinful actions because God searches the heart. Those who fail to seek God's forgiveness are subject to being blotted out of God's book of life (Revelations 3:5). Those of us who fail to forgive others are also subject to being given over to torment (Matthew 18:23-35) and losing God's forgiveness of us.

Is there someone whom you need to forgive? Is it you? Has someone refused to forgive you? Come and lay your wounded self before Abba. Ask Him for His divine intervention and healing.

Matthew 6:14-15, Luke 17:3-4,
Ephesians 4:31-32

⟪ MY REFLECTIONS ⟫

_____

_____

_____

_____

_____

_____

_____

_____

_____

_____

_____

_____

DAY 16

***Healing: The result of being cured; the
process of becoming whole; the act of
being restored to one's original state.***

---

*I shall not die, but live and declare the works
of the Lord. (Colossians 3:13, NIV)*

SOMETIMES GOD GIVES HEALING IMMEDIATELY
and sometimes not at all. It's according to His will...

We see this point illustrated in the interwoven
miracle stories of Jairus and the woman with the
issue of blood. In Mark 5:22-42, Jairus seeks out Jesus
to heal his daughter. While on the way to his house, a
woman with an issue of blood presses through the
crowd and receives a transfer of healing virtue
through one touch. Her healing is quick. It happens
right before Jairus even though he had asked for a
healing touch first. Then his servants come and tell

him that his daughter is dead. Jesus encourages him to fear not but only believe.

When we do not receive immediate healing or when an illness reoccurs, we have to release fear and continue to believe in Him. He is our Jehovah-Rophe, our Healer. He promises that the diseases plaguing the Egyptians will no longer have authority over us (Exodus 15:26).

We must hold on to the work of Jesus Christ in times of prolonged or difficult illnesses. By His stripes, we are healed (Isaiah 53:5). Jesus bore our sins in His body on a tree for us to live to righteousness and thrive in good health (1 Peter 2:24). He promised that the Sun of Righteousness will rise with healing in His wings, and we will be free (Malachi 4:2). It is not God's will for us to be unhealthy or not whole. The infirmity has a purpose, and we must trust in the Lord and know that ultimate healing comes when we return to Heaven to be one with Him (Revelations 21:4; 2 Corinthians 5:8).

Physical illness is a result of the fall of man; nevertheless, God can heal by His divine words, medications, doctors and most importantly, faith in Him. During times of infirmity, we must remember His word. As we make the weekly trek to the hospital for chemotherapy sessions, we must remember that Abba Father told us to fear not because He is with us to strengthen and uphold us with His mighty righteous right hand (Isaiah 41:10).

As pain courses through our bodies or when needles numb our fingers or thighs from the daily monitoring of diabetes, Jeremiah told us that God would bring it to health and healing and reveal an abundance of prosperity and security (Jeremiah 33:6). When we petition God to spare us or a loved one from illness or death and He doesn't do it, we declare and decree that God heals the brokenhearted and binds up their wounds (Psalm 147:3), and we shall have perfect peace if we keep our mind stayed on Him (Isaiah 26:3). What other promises can we stand on during illnesses?

We must remember that the body, soul and spirit are connected, so one affects the other. When our body is sick, we don't feel like praying or studying the word. The discomfort quickens and weakens our flesh, and our minds focus on what is present instead of seeking the presence of God in prayer and scriptures. Our spirit man suffers as we disconnect from the source of life and healing and become our own physicians who dictate when and how we should be healed.

In 2 Kings 5:1-15, Naaman's healing didn't come the way he expected; it came from an unexpected place-- the Jordan River. We should never scoff at how God decides to heal. Naaman may have thought he was too important to dip in the Jordan River but once he humbled himself, his skin became as a child's skin. We can't allow our intellect to block God's hand of healing.

Healing is not only physical; it can be spiritual. Spiritual healing is something that we as believers must really focus on daily. We must examine ourselves for branches that need to be pruned because they are producing unhealthy fruit that stunts spiritual devclopment (John 15:2). What areas of your spiritual health do you need to address?

Matthew 8:14, Luke 13:11-13, James 5:14-18

⟨ᴡ *MY REFLECTIONS* ᴡ⟩

_____

_____

_____

_____

_____

_____

_____

_____

_____

_____

_____

_____

_____

DAY 17

Guilt/Shame: A feeling of responsibility or regret for committing a legal or personal offense; a feeling of humiliation, embarrassment or self-condemnation over a real or perceived wrongful act...

I, even I, am he that blotteth out thy transgressions for mine own sake and will not remember thy sins. (Isaiah 43:25)

THE ENEMY USES FIERY DARTS to attack us daily (Ephesians 6:16). His arsenal includes strongholds, torment and wrong mindsets (2 Corinthians 10:4-5). They are those arrows that fly by day and terrors that come at night (Psalm 91:5). Guilt, shame, bitterness, fear, temptation, gluttony, addictions, covetousness, fornication, self-centeredness, competition and gossip are some of the fiery darts that he manipulates to keep us in bondage and separate us from fellowship with God.

Even things that God initially designs to help us draw nearer to Him, to grow through them and not remain in them or to change them from their original intent, such as sorrow, suffering and self-esteem are at the enemy's disposal to distort as an arrow to wound and weaken us (Romans 8:18; 1 John 5:4-5; 1 Peter 4:12-13).

Whether we have made mistakes, committed sins or condemned ourselves for acts done towards us by others, God doesn't want us to wallow in it like the prodigal son did in the pigpen. It doesn't matter if the guilt/shame originates from being abandoned by a loved one. God still loves us. His love is never-ending. It defeats guilt and shame. His love washes it away (Ezekiel 16:9) as we draw nigh to Him (James 4:8) and reason with Him (Isaiah 1:18). The light and truth of His Spirit and word expose any wrong we have done and call us to repentance, accountability, correction and restoration.

Maybe that is why some of us do not really go deeper in our Bible study besides what we get in church or a daily devotional here or there when time permits. If the word is alive and sharper than a double-edged sword, it will cut deep into issues that we try to cover up.

Can we be courageous enough to lay down under the microscope of God's word so He can search our inward parts and discover truth in them? Can we be transparent and vulnerable with God?

Guilt/shame are kissing cousins; they are so intimately related that they are hard to separate. Once we feel guilt, shame is surely to follow and partner with it. Guilt/shame can be a dark cloud that looms over our lives because of past actions. Once we acknowledge our wrongs and come to grips with it, we can find freedom and peace through God's amazing grace, along with taking responsibility for our own actions.

The first mention of guilt/shame can be found in the Garden of Eden (Genesis 3:1-11). Adam & Eve felt guilt and shame after they ate the forbidden fruit. Before they had committed the offense, they had no prior knowledge of what nakedness was. They were comfortable with being their true selves in God's presence. When a snake entered their land, they became entangled in the manipulation of words, and it separated them from fellowship with God.

What snakes do we have in our land that are causing guilt, shame and separation from God?

Once King David was confronted by Nathan the prophet about his sin with Bathsheba, he repented by asking for forgiveness. He asked God to purge him, create a clean heart in him and restore the joy of his salvation (Psalm 51:10-12). Before Nathan confronted him, David felt like he was right in what he did. Guilt and shame quickly overcame him, but he remembered He had a heavenly Father whom he could talk to and ask for forgiveness and correction. He did not wallow in the guilt and shame; he laid them and himself at the altar.

Lay at the altar today and release your guilt and shame.

Isaiah 61:7, Jeremiah 33:8, Romans 8:1,
1 John 1:9

ᏉᏪ *MY REFLECTIONS* ᏉᏪ

_____

_____

_____

_____

_____

_____

_____

_____

_____

_____

_____

_____

DAY 18

Bitterness: A feeling of anger and disappointment at being treated unfairly and if it is not dealt with properly, it can evolve into a root...

Let all bitterness, and wrath, and anger, and clamour, and evil speaking, be put away from you, with all malice. (Ephesians 4:31)

THE WAY WE RESPOND TO SUFFERING determines whether we become bitter or better. God's grace is sufficient to calm our suffering. We can choose to forgive or dwell upon the wrongdoing. When we discover bitterness has settled in our hearts, we need to realize that it takes a process to get to that point. Anger or disappointment is the seed and from that seed, the branches of resentment come forth.

Our mind replays the hurtful act until it becomes a movie reel. Each time we visit the memory, we relive the pain and the wound gets deeper and deeper. Now the root of bitterness has grown. It bears fruit that poisons and infects. The root of bitterness opens the door for infirmity to come in. If we do not deal with it quickly and properly, it will become a tree that hardens our hearts to the point where we cannot allow any light or truth to penetrate. A hardened heart is one that is devoid of light so it is dark. The more the memory replays, the more it becomes a heart of stone instead of a heart of flesh. The more the memory rests in the forefront of our minds, the more the past becomes a false present that prevents us from being present and moving forward to our future.

When a soldier is engaged in war, he or she may experience post-traumatic stress disorder (PTSD) when their service ends. Their bodies have left the place of battle, but their minds are still there. The scenes of harsh death and destruction surround them. It is like they have placed their phones in a virtual reality device, and the real world has disappeared. They are stuck in a quicksand of memories while the present world is turning on its axis, days turning into nights, people moving forward. It spirals them downward into a tomb of that moment and they can't function in their lives unless they get psychological and spiritual help to lay axe to the root (Matthew 3:10) and bring them into the present to live and not exist. Bitterness is a spiritual post-traumatic stress disorder that steals, kills and destroys us unless we hold on to Jesus' hand and let Him give us life more abundantly.

What is stealing our joy right now? What is preventing us from being present? What is it that we cannot let go?

Our first example of bitterness is in the story of Cain and Abel (Genesis 4:3-16). For whatever reason, God rejected Cain's offering to Him and deemed Abel's sacrifice as more acceptable. God is a God of second, third, fourth to infinity chances. Cain had every opportunity to humble himself, seek God's face and find out what he needed to do to make his offering right unto God. The all-knowing God could see that Cain's anger was escalating into bitterness. He said, "Why art thou wroth? And why is thy countenance fallen? If thou doest well, shalt thou not be accepted? and if thou doest not well, sin lieth at the door. And unto thee shall be his desire, and thou shalt rule over him (Genesis 4:6-7)." The root of bitterness had embedded itself so deeply inside Cain's heart that it led to his brother, Abel's murder and Cain's exile.

Women in the Bible have dealt with the bitterness of life's situations. Hannah could have remained in the bitterness of her soul and given up on her barrenness, but she chose to stay focused on what she wanted and faith prevailed. She was able to overcome shame and ridicule and move on (1 Samuel 1:10-18). Job's wife allowed the loss of her children and possessions to make her bitter and curse God (Job 2:9-10). Naomi experienced bitterness because she lost everything she knew. Naomi even changed her name to Mara which meant "bitterness," and she felt like she left home full and was returning empty (Ruth 1:19-22). Nevertheless, she was restored to a right relationship with God. Not only women have been afflicted with bitterness, but men like Esau and David have also been plagued with it (Genesis 27:37; 2 Samuel 14:12-14, 24).

Sometimes we refuse to acknowledge just how hurt we really are. Being honest with ourselves and God is the path to healing. What do you need to be honest about with yourself and God?

Deuteronomy 29:18-20, Proverbs 17:9, Hebrews 12:14-17

⟪ᴍᴡ MY REFLECTIONS ᴡᴡ⟫

_____

_____

_____

_____

_____

_____

_____

_____

_____

DAY 19

Sorrow: A feeling of deep distress by loss, disappointment or other misfortune suffered by oneself or others...

My soul is weary with sorrow; strengthen me according to your word. (Psalm 119:28 NIV)

SORROW IS MORE THAN AN EMOTION; it is a living being that sits with us and tries to befriend us. Sorrow changes our names, identities and outlook on life. It can lead us into a dark pit that only the comfort of the Holy Spirit and time can bring us out. Singers and poets express their sorrows through their art as a way of release. Billie Holiday aka "Lady Day" has a song called "Good Morning, Heartache" in which she invites her sorrow to sit down with her. Dorothy Parker lamented over her sorrow in poetry and compared it to a fresh, eternal place of agony.

91

The world deals with sorrow differently than the believers of Jesus Christ. Yes, we go through the process of mourning and loss. For example, many women experience sorrow over their barrenness in childbirth. Some people go through the death of a loved one, divorce, job loss and other life events. We all experience sorrow at some time in our lives. But we as believers stand on the promise that God's grace is sufficient for every situation (2 Corinthians 12:9-10).

We realize that weeping may endure for a moment, but joy will come in the morning (Psalm 30:5). Our God promises that He is the God of comfort who will comfort us in all our affliction so that we may comfort others (2 Corinthians 1:3-4). When sorrow and grief overwhelm us, the Lord draws near to our broken hearts and saves us when we are crushed in spirit (Psalm 34:18). He is a battleax in the time of a battle, even when that battle is getting the strength to get out of the bed and eat when all we want to do is pull the covers over our heads. He is the lifter of our heads as He comes in strong and mighty in the battle (Psalm 24:7-8), rolling away the garment of sorrow and surrounding us with His peace. We are blessed when we mourn because we will be comforted (Matthew 5:4), and when our flesh and heart fail, we can just hold on to God as the strength of our hearts and our portion forever (Psalm 73:26).

Oh, with tears in our eyes and weakness in our limbs, we utter praises and promises through our weeping knowing that He will make it better in due time.

What other promises of God can we meditate on when we are dealing with sorrow?

Leah knew sorrow well (Genesis 29:16-35). She loved a man who didn't love her back. She was trapped in a marriage where she did everything she could to please him, but he still desired another woman, her sister. God showed favor toward her by opening her womb. With each birth, sorrow caused her to seek her husband's approval instead of thanking God for His grace. Leah got the point when Judah was born. The word of the Lord says, "She conceived again, and when she gave birth to a son she said, 'This time I will praise the LORD.' So, she named him Judah (Genesis 29:35)."

Godly sorrow is different from grief because it leads to repentance. It comes from man transgressing God's words or a remorse from disappointing God Himself, our loving Father. We just talked about remembering the promises of God, but we must also remember that those promises come with an accountability to purify ourselves from anything that contaminates our body and prevents us from being holy unto God (2 Corinthians 7:1). Later in verses 9-11 of the same chapter, Paul tells the Corinthians how godly sorrow not only produces repentance, but it processes us into a higher level in our walk with God.

More importantly, as believers we should sorrow over the barrenness of the lost souls to the point of trying to win them to Christ. It is the great commission our Savior has bestowed upon us. We are not here on earth just to live out our lives. We have a mantle of evangelism that we must put into action.

How are you winning souls for Christ? Are you grieving over the lost or judging and condemning them?

Isaiah 53:4-5, Isaiah 60:1-3, Romans 15:1-6, 1 Corinthians15:54-58

⟵ *MY REFLECTIONS* ⟶

_____

_____

_____

_____

_____

_____

_____

_____

_____

_____

DAY 20

Fear: A feeling of danger or being frightful; a spirit of timidity that causes us to leave God out and run away from our challenges; a feeling that enables us to not walk in our true identities...

For God hath not given us the spirit of fear; but of power, and of love, and of a sound mind. (2 Timothy 1:7)

CHILD OF GOD, did you not know that your Father has said, that there is no fear in love; but perfect love casts out fear: because fear has torment. He that fears is not made perfect in love (1 John 4:18)? Therefore, beloved, release the fear and wrap yourself in His love.

Child of God, did you not know that your Lord has said to fear not for He is your shield and exceeding great reward (Genesis 15:1)? Take up your shield of faith and quench that fiery dart of fear.

Child of God, remember what He promised you. You are of God, His precious child. You have already overcome because the Greater One lives in you and He is greater than he that is in the world (1 John 4:4). So, put the enemy back in his rightful place—beneath your feet.

Child of God, hold your head up high, stand still and see the salvation of the Lord. Whatever your Egyptians may be, you will never see them again (Exodus 14:13). Help is on the way. Stop fretting and praise Him!

Child of God, did you not know that your confidence and boldness is in Him? For He promised you that if you praise His word and place your trust in Him, you will have no need to fear what flesh can do unto you (Psalm 56:4)?

Therefore, let go of the fear of man and increase your reverent fear of the Lord Almighty. Is He not the Lord Almighty? Is He not the worthy Lamb?

The best promise is the one found in our key verse. We should read it in every translation possible so we can come to a deeper understanding of what our Father says. Fear is a strong, feisty spirit that is at the root of many afflictions and spiritual warfare. It will paralyze, silence and kill our witness to the power of the Almighty God. It will convince us to run away from our purpose and go into hiding like Elijah did in 1 Kings 19.

Fear will cause us to settle for comfortability or mediocrity instead of embracing the strange and unfamiliar like when the disciples in the boat refuse to follow Peter out on the water. It will make us hide in the darkness when we are supposed to be the light because we are afraid of what others will think like Nicodemus when he sought out the Truth.

Fear is one of the battles that we as believers constantly face. We did not suffer and come out of battle without our war stories. Our battles and testimonies are for those that come after us as well as those that are still in a war. We must keep in mind that God is always with us; we just need to ask Him to make us aware of His presence (Isaiah 41:10). Barak exhibits fear of battle without Deborah in Judges 4:4-9, but God had already predestined his inheritance. God said He would never leave us nor forsake us. Our faith must be bigger than our fear.

Joshua had every right to be fearful. He was following the footsteps of his mentor, Moses. This man walked in the glory of God and had allowed God to use Him to do some of the greatest miracles in the Bible. He also dealt with generations of a people who struggled to maintain their trust and submission to God. However, God was with him just like He was with Moses. In Joshua 1:1-9, God reassures Joshua three times to be strong and courageous as he operated in the call on his life. We should meditate on these verses and place our names in them when we feel fear trying to rise in us.

The fear of the Lord should be the only fear that we possess. When we exalt Him, we make Him bigger than whatever is worrying or frightening us. When we remind God of who He is instead of reminding Him of our problems, we invite Him in. We give too much power to our fears. We must remember the One who has all power. He requires us to fear Him in Deuteronomy 10:12. Ask the Lord to deliver you from fear and increase the fear of Him in you today.

Psalm 23:4, Psalm 49:5, Psalm 139:1-6, Matthew 6:25

⟨w MY REFLECTIONS w⟩

DAY 21

Temptation: A feeling of strong desire
to have or do something that does not
align with God's will...

Blessed is the man that endureth temptation:
for when he is tried, he shall receive the crown
of life, which the Lord hath promised to them
that love him. (James 1:12)

As BELIEVERS WE'RE SURROUNDED by temptation every day. When we file our taxes, there is a temptation to not report every bit of income to avoid paying the IRS. We are tempted to omit little details in a conversation or a job application when omission is as much of a lie as telling an untruth. When we are surrounded by gossip in the church pews before service or in the company breakroom, we have a strong desire to stay and listen or jump into the conversation. When our flesh speaks louder

101

than our spirit or sleep convinces us to stay in bed on Sunday morning or we take a friendship with the opposite sex further into adultery, we have fallen into temptation.

Temptation is the desire to act upon something that goes against God's word and will produce a work of the flesh. It is an action that leads to sin, and as James 1:15 states, it will lead to death. Temptation can be as simple as overeating to the point of gluttony when we see an enticing buffet of food. It could be the temptation to get angry with the driver who cut us off in traffic and say unkind words or even use profanity. Perhaps it is a desire to retaliate or exchange words with someone who has offended us. No matter what the entrapment may be, God gives us a way of escape in 1 Corinthians 10:13, and James exhorts us to resist the devil and he will flee (4:7).

In 1 Samuel 24:1-22, David and his men are hiding in the cave of En Gedi. King Saul entered the cave to relieve himself and did not see them. David's men told him that the Lord had given David's enemy to do as he wished. David cut a piece of King Saul's robe, but his conscience bothered him. David was a man whose heart panted after God. He always stayed in His presence and inquired of Him on what to do. The temptation was so great that David could not hear God's voice. God didn't tell him to attack King Saul; his men did. The Holy Spirit convicted him.

How many times have we allowed the voice of man to be louder in our ears than God's voice? When was the last time that the Holy Spirit convicted us about something? Has sin deafened our spiritual ears or numbed us so much that we can't feel the conviction anymore?

King David told his men, "The Lord forbid that I should do such a thing to my master, the Lord's anointed, or lay my hand on him; for he is the anointed of the Lord (v.6, NIV)." He followed King Saul out of the cave and shared with him how he had an opportunity to kill him, but he showed self-control and resisted the temptation. He remembered that vengeance and judgment were the Lord's, and he had no right to judge or exact vengeance against King Saul. In verse 15, David let King Saul know who the final judge was when he said, "May the Lord be our judge and decide between us. May he consider my cause and uphold it; may he vindicate me by delivering me from your hand (NIV)." David realized that even though King Saul had lost his mind and wrongfully pursued him, he could not touch God's anointed.

Each of us have an anointing on our lives, especially those who are called to preach the word of the Lord. We must resist the temptation to put our mouths on anointed pastors and ministry leaders. When we speak against them, assassinate their characters or slander them, we are in error. Even when we yield to the temptation to speak against our spiritual brothers and sisters, we are coming against God's anointed. God sees all and knows all, and He is also the One who anointed them in the first place. He is the final judge and has the final say, not us.

David was also God's anointed and during his kingship, he fell into temptation. He slept with Bathsheba even after men told him that she was Uriah's wife. His failure to resist temptation cost him greatly, especially in his family.

What will it cost us if we yield to sin? Will our families, jobs, health, reputations or social standing suffer? Is it worth it? Remember Jesus' response when He faced the devil's temptation in the wilderness: It is written (Matthew 4:1-11). Fill up on the Word daily so you can pray and confess it when temptation comes.

Judges 16:5, Proverbs 6:20-24, Mark 14:38, James 1:2-4

⟪ MY REFLECTIONS ⟫

_____

_____

_____

_____

_____

_____

_____

_____

_____

DAY 22

Gluttony: A mental or emotional behavior that results in habitual greed or excess in eating or drinking...

For the drunkard and the glutton shall come to poverty: and drowsiness shall clothe a man with rags. (Proverbs 23:21)

GLUTTONY CANNOT BE SATISFIED. It is an out-of-control appetite for food or drinking. It is to food what greed is to material wealth. Gluttony can lead to obesity and other health problems, and sometimes can be traced to emotional issues. Solomon said if we are given to appetite, it is best to put a knife to our throats (Proverbs 23:1-2). Now Solomon doesn't mean this literally, but he is talking about having self-control and letting all things be done in moderation (Philippians 4:4). We must remember that our bodies are to bring glory to God (1 Corinthians 6:20), and not to satisfy our harmful and selfish appetites.

When we think of greed, the word insatiable comes to mind. It is a desire that can never be filled. We eat that one piece of chocolate or that spoonful of ice cream. Then it escalates to a gallon of ice cream a week or a constant stream of sweets, snacks and any other type of food entering our bodies without being really conscious of what we are doing. Those who love to drink can't stop with one glass of wine or one beer. The taste whets their appetites, and they must have one after the other until they have impaired their senses and judgment. We need to hunger and thirst for the things of God, for we shall continually be filled (Matthew 5:6).

As Solomon notes in our key verse, the drunkard and the glutton shall come to poverty. Think about it. If we love Coca Cola or other soda products or even coffee, we are consistently trying to find change or swiping our cards because we "got" to have it. If we really track how much we spend on coffee or soda or eating out, we would probably have enough to pay off debts that we are praying to the Lord to provide financially in a supernatural way. If we eat or drink too much, drowsiness consumes us and we lose focus on our divine assignments. Then we are out-of-place and out-of-order because our appetites are out-of-control. We become enslaved to things that God formed first as preparation for our nourishment, not overconsumption (Genesis 1:29). We have allowed food and drink to dominate us when we have been given dominion (Genesis 1:26-28; Genesis 2:15).

There is a term that chefs use, and it is called "comfort food." There are foods that our grandparents, parents or loved ones have made that make us feel warm and at ease when we eat them. There is nothing wrong with that. The problem comes when we substitute the comfort of food for the comfort of God.

Feeling stressed or pressured? Are you drowning in life's issues? Don't pick up food or drink, pick up the Word.

Then should I yet have comfort; yea, I would harden myself in sorrow: let him not spare; for I have not concealed the words of the Holy One (Job 6:10). Finding comfort in food and drink hardens our hearts from receiving the water of the word.

Yeah, though I walk through the valley of the shadow of death, I will fear no evil: for thou art with me; thy rod and thy staff they comfort me (Psalm 23:4). Find comfort in Him only. Fear not, faith only.

Break forth into joy, sing together, ye waste places of Jerusalem: for the Lord hath comforted his people, he hath redeemed Jerusalem (Isaiah 52:9). Let the overflow of the Spirit give you ease, not gluttonous behaviors.

Wherefore comfort yourselves together, and edify one another, even as also ye do (1 Thessalonians

5:11). Seek the assembly of believers, not food or drink.

If we really think about it, overconsumption of anything besides food or alcohol can be gluttony because greed is at the root of it. When an insatiable hunger or thirst for something rules our lives, it becomes our god and we cross the line into idolatry. Have you made food your god? What or whom is the god/God of your life?

Psalm 78:18, Proverbs 25:19, Ephesians 5:18, Philippians 3:19

ᛜ MY REFLECTIONS ᛜ

_____

_____

_____

_____

_____

_____

_____

_____

_____

_____

_____

DAY 23

Addiction: A physical or mental dependence on a substance or activity and an inability to stop engaging with it; being a slave to a negative habit; a spiritual form of bondage that hinders us from being free...

For all that is in the world, the lust of the flesh, and the lust of the eyes, and the pride of life, is not of the Father, but is of the world. (1 John 2:16)

WHEN WOMEN ARE PREGNANT, they have cravings for different types of foods and other edible treats. Some may eat foods they have never liked or tried before. A whiff of the aroma enters our noses, and the babies in our wombs start moving to let us know----hey, I want some of that, and I want it now! If we do not get it into our bellies soon, we will not be satisfied until we get it.

111

When a swimmer or surfer has a bleeding injury, the scent of blood immediately attracts the shark. It activates the sensory part of its brain and signals that food or prey is near. The shark is overcome with a strong desire to seek, find and consume this prey. Its eyes even turn black with no depths. The shark's movements become frenzied. It destroys anything and anyone in its path until it gets what it wants. If it consumes its prey and another scent of blood arises, it will continue to feed. It knows no limits.

There has been an influx of internet cafés popping up in strip malls and neighborhoods across the country. These businesses are really casinos in which people line up early in the morning to wait for the doors to open. They stay in the building all day and night. Maybe they will get lucky, but they are not being good stewards of their money, time or talents in this environment. They have become addicted to the luck of the draw.

Addiction is just like that. The scent or taste of the drug or alcohol makes the addicted lose their minds. They steal from loved ones and risk the destruction of relationships and families to get one hit. The addiction can be more than drugs or alcohol. It can be social media, technology, shopping, profanity, money, power, material things, gambling or sex. If it feeds our flesh to the point that we have no self-control to stop in our own strength, it's an addiction.

Addiction is a deadly dance with a spirit that controls us like a puppet.

Addiction is more than a bad habit, but it is an uncontrollable, constant urge. Most people may not even want it, but the addiction is insistent as it produces an overpowering bondage. It begins with a fascination. Temptation yields to the desire, and the desire becomes a priority in our lives. The issue must be confessed to God and the desire to be free must become priority. We must realize we have an addiction before we can be delivered. Denying it keeps us in bondage, and bondage is not God's will.

King Solomon is a biblical example of someone who dealt with an addiction to women. 1 Kings 3-10 shows him to be a righteous heir to his father David's throne. Even though his brother, Adonijah tried to take the throne from him, King Solomon became king at a very young age. He pursued the heart of God like his father David. He asked for wisdom, and God blessed him abundantly with that and so much more. Also like his father, King Solomon had a weakness for women and a strong bondage to lust.

Right after great accomplishments, the enemy will pinpoint a perforation in the hedge to try to assassinate the call God has on our lives. We must always be prayerful.

King Solomon had just completed building the temple and hearkened the people to humble themselves, seek God so that He may heal their land (2 Chronicles 7:4-16). The queen of Sheba blessed him with extravagant gifts and had just praised his walk into the house of God. However, he loved many strange women from nations God specifically told them not to associate with, and his heart was not perfect with God because he worshipped the many gods of his wives and concubines (1 Kings

11:1-4). Addictions redirect our love to something other than God. We come out of alignment with God's control and fall under the control of a created thing that has no eyes, no mouth and no power. What addictions do you need to give up? Do you have a loved one struggling with addiction? Pray about it.

Leviticus 26:1, 1 Corinthians 6:12,
Galatians 5:1

ᔰ *MY REFLECTIONS* ᔰ

_____

_____

_____

_____

_____

_____

_____

_____

_____

_____

_____

_____

_____

DAY 24

Covetousness: The feeling of having or showing great desire to possess something belonging to someone else...

And he said unto them, Take heed, and beware of covetousness: for a man's life consisteth not in the abundance of the things which he possesseth. (Luke 12:15)

SEEK YE FIRST THE KINGDOM OF GOD and His righteousness, and all these things shall be added to you.

Matthew 6:33 is quoted often by believers, but some of us really do not understand the true meaning of this promise. It is not an entitlement clause that we can use to justify why we deserve something. It does not mean that God will always give us what we want.

It certainly doesn't mean that if someone else has it we should have it, too.

When you seek the things of God, the things of the world do not matter; they become secondary.

However, the society we live in says we must have more, more and more. We must look the part and keep up with the Joneses. Less is an option. We are bombarded with thoughts of not having enough. Covetousness is not only a desire to possess material possessions or wealth; it's also a strong desire to have other people's spouses, positions, gifts or anointings.

We can even covet the things of God. Now there is a difference between being zealous and being covetous. Being zealous is when we are so on fire for God that we truly enjoy pleasing Him through service, relationship and discipleship. We seek His applause, heart and agenda, and not man's. Being covetous is the complete opposite. It means we are seeking the things of God to obtain the glory of men or to satisfy selfish ambition.

Simon the sorcerer coveted the gift of the Holy Spirit after watching Peter lay hands on the people (Acts 8:9-24). Before he accepted salvation, Simon manipulated people through witchcraft and received so much acclaim and honor from them. He figured that if he could buy this divine power, he could be even more prosperous and powerful. His soul was saved, but it wasn't renewed. Peter rebuked him and urged him to repent.

We can trace covetousness back to the enemy and see its influence throughout the Bible. The adversary desired to possess God's position, power and influence, and his bright morning star fell from heaven and turned into utter darkness and evil. Then covetousness slithered into the Garden of Eden and convinced Adam & Eve that what God reserved for Himself should belong to them. Jacob coveted Esau's birthright and blessing. The church at Corinth coveted certain gifts over others to the point that it caused dissension. Paul taught them in 1 Corinthians 12-14 that love was the more excellent way and the choicest of graces and all gifts are to edify the church, not to divide it.

Jezebel murdered Naboth because Ahab wanted his vineyard and Naboth told him no (1 Kings 21:1-16). Korah coveted Moses and Aaron's influence and authority (Numbers16:1-5). He didn't realize the sacrifice and journey Moses and Aaron continually endured to walk in that call. King David not only committed adultery and murder, but he also walked in covetousness. He had people, power and prosperity. In 2 Samuel 12:1-14, God used Nathan as His mouthpiece to release a convicting message through a parable. God had given David everything, but his covetous desire for Bathsheba, another man's wife, made it seem like God didn't give him enough. In 2 Samuel 12:8, God said, "If this had not been too little, I also would have given you much more."

We must counter covetousness with gratitude. God has blessed us with so much. He knows what we can handle. We must learn to trust Him with our whole heart and not lean on our understanding in which we believe we should have what others possess. Don't think about what you don't have today. Offer God a sacrifice of thanksgiving that gives Him glory (Psalm 50:23).

Are there any areas in your life where covetousness may be abounding? How can you show more gratitude for what God has done?

Exodus 20:17, Luke 12:15-21, Ephesians 5:5, Hebrews 13:5

⟵ MY REFLECTIONS ⟶

_____

_____

_____

_____

_____

_____

_____

_____

_____

_____

_____

DAY 25

---

*Fornication: The act of sexual
intercourse between people who are
unmarried...*

---

*Flee fornication. Every sin that a man doeth is
without the body; but he that committeth
fornication sinneth against his own body. (1
Corinthians 6:18)*

Culture says: You're so old-fashioned. No one
                           waits until they get married
                           anymore.

Counterculture says: My body is not for fornication, but
                           for the Lord and the Lord is for my
                           body (1 Corinthians 6:13). Because
                           I am His child, I must obey His
                           word.

Culture says:	You would do this if you really loved me.
Counterculture says:	I can only love in deed and truth that honor God (1 John 3:18). Because I love Him, I must keep His commandments (John 14:15).
Culture says:	Why buy the cow when you can get the milk for free?
Counterculture says:	I have been called to holiness and not impurity (1 Thessalonians 4:7). Because I worship Him, I must be a living sacrifice that shows His good, acceptable and perfect will (Romans 12:1-2).

TODAY'S CULTURE ADVOCATES living together in fornication. It teaches us that we are in control of our bodies, and we have the right to make decisions on what to do with them. Some people even believe that living together is a good way to test drive each other for compatibility. Abstinence is a taboo word that brings ridicule in a world where self-gratification rules.

Culture has a voice that is strong and convincing. It carries popular opinion and influences the spheres of entertainment, education and governmental systems. However, we are a part of a royal government whose kingdom has no end. We as believers are called to be the counterculture just like Jesus.

As God's children, we are called to a higher standard of living that is governed by His word.

Fornication is a temptation that every man and woman has faced in his or her life. It is a real force to be reckoned with.as the flesh lusts against the spirit and the spirit lusts against the flesh (Galatians 5:17). It is a constant battle that plagues believers. We were called to live a life as chaste, holy vessels (2 Corinthians 11:2).

Chastity means abstaining from sexual activity because we know our bodies are the temples of the Holy Spirit. Paul says if the married cannot exercise self-control, let them marry. It's better to marry than to burn with passion (1 Corinthians 7:8).

God will not give us desires that cannot be contained according to His standards of holiness. We must guard our eye gates and ear gates to avoid temptation. Although the desire for sex is natural and healthy in the original intent that God created it to be, its fulfillment cannot be found everywhere.

In John 4:4-29, Jesus went against culture and stopped in Samaria. He needed to see a woman who had been seeking fulfillment in men. Culture said for Jews to dissociate themselves from Samaritans. Counterculture said that He came to gather His lost sheep and teach them the true meaning of worship and spiritual fulfillment. When we worship God in spirit and truth, we realize that pursuing the heart of God is better than gratifying the flesh.

If you are struggling with the temptation of fornication, ask the Holy Spirit to strengthen you with might in your inner man. Think about today's generation. How can you convince them that it is worth the wait?

Exodus 20:17, Matthew 15:19, Ephesians 5:5

⋘ MY REFLECTIONS ⋙

_____

_____

_____

_____

_____

_____

_____

_____

_____

_____

_____

_____

_____

DAY 26

Self-centeredness: An egotistical behavior in which one is solely concerned with one's own interests or agenda...

Let nothing be done through strife or vainglory; but in lowliness of mind let each esteem other better than themselves. (Philippians 2:3)

"I'M DOING ME," is a common phrase in popular culture. It is all about the self and what it wants. Self-centeredness is getting what one desires by any means necessary with no regard to whomever is in the way. It derives from a sense of entitlement and narcissism. Self-centeredness is a fruit of the flesh that violates God's commandment "to love your neighbor as yourself. (Mark 12:31)."

It even afflicts us believers in the church. On Sunday mornings, there are some people who feel like their favorite seat is their spot. If anyone sits there, they will stand firmly and quietly or cause a scene until they get their seat back. It may happen in ministry. A servant's heart can quickly transform into a selfish heart when he or she is more interested in things being done his or her way instead of God's way. Have we become self-centered in our serving?

Focusing on our flesh opens us up to temptation, pride, envy, boasting, lying and all manner of evil. We lack dependence in God. We become our own god. This mindset leads to utter destruction. Self-centered people think that their power, strength and might are more influential than God's wisdom.

In the Bible, writers like Jeremiah describe "the arm of flesh" or "the arm of man." In Jeremiah 17:5-6, the Lord said that we become cursed when we trust in man and make flesh our arm [strength] and turn our hearts from God. Instead of being a tree planted by waters that bear fruit because we trust the Lord's righteous right hand (Jeremiah 17:7-8), our lands and lives transform into parched, dry and barren areas. It affects everyone connected to us.

Pharaoh ruled the Israelites by his arm of flesh. With each plague, his heart hardened and he refused to let God's people go. In the scriptures we read that the Lord hardened his heart. The hardness was already there; the Lord just used it to fulfill His plan. Pharaoh's self-centeredness stemmed from rebellion, pride and idolatry. He thought that he was Israel's god. God said in Exodus 9:16-17, "But indeed for this very reason I have allowed you to live, in order to show you My power and in order that My name may be proclaimed throughout all the earth...you are still [arrogantly] exalting yourself [in defiance] against My people by not letting them go (AMP)." Pharaoh's self-centeredness caused his people to lose their firstborn and their lives.

Are we so fixed on our agendas that we have become blinded to the destruction and confusion they are causing?

No matter how hard our hearts may be like fallow ground, how closed off our will is like leviathan's scales (Job 41:15-17), how strong our might or strength may be like iron and brass, God is the all-powerful God. He will perform a demonstration to humble us and prove Himself strong.

Jezebel cared about only herself. Her self-centeredness led to the slaughter of several prophets in her kingdom, witchcraft, oppression and even the murder of Naboth. Her threats, mere words, terrorized Elijah to the point of isolation, depression and the thought of suicide. Her words almost killed his destiny. There was nothing she would not do and no one she would not kill to satisfy her fleshly desires. She thought she was a god and the gods she served possessed total control. El Elyon, the Most God, performed such a demonstration of His sovereignty by being a God who answered by fire. He also declared that her death would be deadly and demeaning (2 Kings 9:9-10, 30-34).

Will we kill others with our words? Will we build or destroy in the body of Christ? Remember our attitude determines our altitude. When we trust in God, our will belongs to Him. Our focus should be on the eternal, not the temporal. Humility is the antidote to self-centeredness. Humble yourself before Him today.

Psalm 86:8-10, Luke 9:23, 1 Corinthians 3:1-3

ᚹ *MY REFLECTIONS* ᚹ

DAY 27

Competition: The activity of striving to gain or win something through defeat or the act of showing superiority over others; one's ambition to pursue a place of honor or victory that exalts one over another...

For just as each of us has one body with many members, and these members do not all have the same function, so in Christ we, though many, form one body, and each member belongs to all the others. We have different gifts, according to the grace given to each of us. (Romans 12:4-6, NIV)

STAY IN YOUR LANE. We often hear this phrase when we are driving. Our fellow drivers may be distracted and drift in our lanes or may be overly aggressive and force their way in front of us. We also use this phrase to describe people who want to copy or do what others are doing, but they do not have the grace or anointing for it.

There is no need to jump in other people's lanes if God's purpose is your road map. What He ordains you to do, no one can take away from you. If God anointed the Israelites to possess a promised land and made waters as a wall, why do we compete against people for a God-created assignment?

Competition can be good if it pushes us in a positive direction to do better. It's sin when we start to destroy others. Competition is not acceptable to God. We are one body, but many members that fit jointly together working in sync for the common good. We should really compete against ourselves to be a better reflection of God's image and standard. Competition leads to comparison, and comparison is sliding down that slippery slope of sin that turns our focus from God to the flesh.

Have we been comparing ourselves to each other recently? What message do we send to non-believers when they see us engaged in unhealthy competition?

Competition occurs throughout the Bible. Martha and Mary were on the same page until Martha started comparing gifts and complaining about Mary not helping (Luke 10:37-42). We are to be of one mind.

Judah and Tamar's twins battled in the womb for the position of firstborn. A red scarlet thread settled the competition. "So, the midwife took a scarlet thread and tied it on his wrist and said, "This one came out first." But when he drew back his hand, his brother came out, and she said, "So this is how you have broken out!" And he was named Perez (Genesis 38: 28-29, NIV). There is no need for us to compete when we all have overcome by the blood of the Lamb.

The sons of Zebedee competed for the place of sitting at the right hand of Jesus in heaven (Matthew 20:20-23). A mother's desire seemed like a good thing. Who wouldn't want their children to have a position of honor? Before we compete or ask for a position, we need to be certain if we can handle the cup. Can we really be broken and endure the warfare that is tied to the next level? Are we ready?

Hananiah competed against Jeremiah's prophecy and tried to tell the people that it would not take them 70 years to escape Babylonian exile. God told him that it would take two years. Hananiah died two years later and Jeremiah's prophecy proved to be true (Jeremiah 28:1-17). Competition can tempt us to manipulate truth to obtain people's praise. We must operate in the truth of who we are.

The sons of Sceva competed with Paul in casting out demons under the authority of the Holy Ghost (Acts 19:13-16). They encountered an evil spirit who didn't know them, and it overpowered them. If we don't have the anointing of Jesus Christ, we can't have the authority over the power of the enemy.

Competition is a divisive tool that works against the body of Christ. How can we celebrate each other instead of competing against each other?

Matthew 19:30, 1 Corinthians 12:7, 11-27, Galatians 6:4, Ephesians 4:3

ᜎᜌᜎ MY REFLECTIONS ᜎᜌᜎ

_____

_____

_____

_____

_____

_____

_____

_____

_____

_____

_____

_____

_____

_____

DAY 28

Gossip: An opportunity where information is shared with negative intention regarding a person...

Keep thy tongue from evil, and thy lips from speaking guile. (Psalm 34:13)

IF DEATH AND LIFE ARE IN THE POWER of the tongue and we eat the fruit of our tongues...

If the words of the Lord framed the world and He spoke everything into existence...

If we decree a thing [exercising our tongues to speak words] and it is established...

If we can be justified or condemned for our words....

If we will have to give an account of our words on the day of judgment...

136

Then why do we participate in gossip? Do we not know that a gossip or a false witness is one that the Lord hates (Proverbs 6:19)? Do we realize that malicious words can murder a person's character, integrity or reputation? However, most of us have gossiped, listened to it or been a victim of it.

Spreading anything that does not help edify a person may be considered as gossip. A mature Christian will exercise control over his or her tongue (James 1:26). It takes the power of the Holy Spirit and a renewed mind to tame our tongues and refrain from gossip. The tongue is a small member but can start fires, cause encouragement or build others up. Gossip is never kind, and we must choose our words carefully.

Listening to gossip is just as bad as spreading it. Imagine if we stood by and watched a man murder someone without calling the police or trying to help. We didn't hold the weapon or act as an accomplice in the crime. Our inaction didn't stop it, either. Our refusal to act condoned what happened. Our silent presence in the middle of gossip speaks loudly to God. We must learn how to disassociate ourselves from it and lovingly rebuke our brothers and sisters who willingly participate in it.

In 1 Samuel 24:9-10, David couldn't understand why Saul let gossip enrage him to the point of trying to kill him. He asked Saul, ""Why do you listen to the people who say I am trying to harm you? This very day you have seen it isn't true. For the Lord placed you at my mercy back there in the cave, and some of my men told me to kill you, but I spared you. For I said, 'I will never harm him—he is the Lord's chosen king' (The Living Bible translation)."

David had served Saul in humility and submission. He fought battles that Saul was too afraid to fight. David soothed the evil spirits that tormented Saul. He lived an upright life before the Lord and did not say one negative word against Saul. Even when Saul died in battle, David mourned and then rebuked the Amalekite who boasted of taking Saul's life (2 Samuel 1:1-17). David responded to Saul's death in a righteous manner that glorified God.

The blind man in John 9:1-23, the man possessed by the legion of demons in Mark 5:1-20 and the woman caught in adultery in John 8:1-11 dealt with gossip about their conditions. Neither the blind man nor his parents committed any sin, but the people spread rumors implying that was the case. They passed by him at the pool where he sat in the same place and condition with no expectation to change. They didn't offer him a hand, only a harsh tongue. The demon-possessed man retreated to the place of the dead, rattled chains, screamed in torment and cut himself. The people talked about him, but they didn't try to help him. Instead of speaking a word into the adulterous woman, the people spoke words of condemnation and murder against her.

When Jesus entered their lives, they were healed, forgiven and transformed into new creations. Jesus often sat in the company of the Pharisees and never participated in the conversation or gossip about what someone had done. If we flip through the scriptures, we would remember Mary Magdalene, Zacchaeus, Matthew, the woman with the alabaster box and countless others. The people were quick to bring up their wrongs and disqualifications, but Jesus saw them as His lost sheep whom He loved so much.

Gossip hurts and maligns. We must look within ourselves to see how we can stop being a part of it, verbally or nonverbally.

Proverbs 19:5, Matthew 15:19, 1 Timothy 3:11

ᐊᵐ MY REFLECTIONS ᵐᐅ

_____

_____

_____

_____

_____

_____

_____

_____

_____

_____

_____

DAY 29

**Suffering: An event or a succession of
events that causes one to experience
pain, distress or sadness; an act or a
season orchestrated by God to build
endurance and draw one closer to Him...**

---

*If we suffer, we shall also reign with him. (2
Timothy 2:12)*

MILLIONS OF CHILDREN IN THE WORLD live with
no clean water or abundant food supply. They are
malnourished as they watch loved ones die of hunger
and thirst.

A family watches a parent go through the stages of
dying in hospice. The mother moans in such agony
and refuses to eat. She sleeps most of the time and
when awakened, the mother forgets the names of the
living, but calls out to people who have already died.

The family wrestles with the agony of her suffering and the overwhelming fear of losing their mother.

A child walks in from school every day with his head bent low. He carries the weight of every shove, tease and hit. He tries everything to make himself smaller, less noticeable, or just plain invisible. The boy has reached out to teachers and his parents; he even whispered a prayer or two to his grandmama's God. His suffering persists. If things do not change soon, if the pressure isn't somehow released, he will have to take matters or his life in his own hands.

Suffering can take us to dark places devoid of hope. It knows no age, location, race or gender, and it is no respecter of persons. Suffering affects everybody at some point in their lives. The world views suffering as a negative consequence due to a wrong decision or punishment for wrongdoing. People often think that a life of suffering isn't normal. It seems dysfunctional. If suffering is always there, then people begin to wonder if they will ever experience happiness.

It is like that dark cloud of dust that always followed the Peanuts character, Pigpen. In cartoons, we may remember a character who had a rain cloud that continuously poured out storms on him wherever he went. Our emotions and intellect make us believe that suffering is an ominous cycle that refuses to release us, but that is not true. As citizens of heaven, the peculiar ones, we must accept the call to suffering.

The question we must ask ourselves is this: will it make us bitter or better?

No one wants to suffer, but we pray to be more like Christ. To be like Him means we're not exempted from losing loved ones, jobs or homes. We will have illnesses that affect our health. These challenges teach us that God's grace is enough, and they build up our resilience.

Suffering can be a measuring tool for evaluating our growth. Do we learn from it, or is it a setback? Do we whine, or is it an opportunity to reflect on the underlying lesson? Can anyone see what the Lord is doing in our lives, or more importantly, can we see what God is doing?

Paul asked the Lord three times for deliverance from suffering caused by a thorn in his flesh (2 Corinthians 12:7-8). The thorn helped him to understand how important it is to draw from the reservoir of God's strength in his weakness. If he had experienced the great visions and didn't receive the thorn (2 Corinthians 12:1-7), Paul could have become prideful or self-righteous.

Paul learned about the power of suffering and its validation of his qualification to serve as an apostle of the Lord. In 2 Corinthians 11:1-29, some of the members of the Corinthian congregation challenged Paul's authority. He developed a resume of his sufferings. He said, "If I must boast, I will boast of the things that show my weakness. The God and Father of the Lord Jesus, who is to be praised forever, knows that I am not lying (2 Corinthians 11:30-31)." There is power in moments of weakness, and that power is the demonstration of the Holy Spirit empowering us to make it through the difficult times. Will you let your suffering defeat you or develop you?

Judges 11:29-40, 2 Samuel 13:1-22, Job 7:1-21

⟨⟨ *MY REFLECTIONS* ⟩⟩

_____

_____

_____

_____

_____

_____

_____

_____

_____

_____

_____

_____

_____

_____

_____

DAY 30

Self-esteem: A positive, healthy confidence in one's own worth or abilities; our true identity that is based on what God says about us, not man....

I will praise thee; for I am fearfully and wonderfully made: marvellous are thy works; and that my soul knoweth right well. (Psalm 139:14)

LOW SELF-ESTEEM STARTS AT AN EARLY AGE in girls. Media, peer pressure and bullying can add to the pressure of young women not loving themselves. It can lead to toxic relationships that are based on affirmation from others. Boys are not exempt from low-self-esteem, either. They struggle with not liking or loving themselves. Boys just carry it inside more because society has unfortunately told them that they must demonstrate strength and emotions are a sign of weakness. As they mature into young women and men, they need to know what their Heavenly Father says about them. We need to know, too.

He declares that we are of more value than the sparrows (Luke 12:7). In Song of Solomon 4:7, the Lord says that we are altogether beautiful, my darling; there is no flaw in us, but we spend so much time pointing out what we do not like about ourselves outwardly and inwardly. God formed us in our mothers' wombs and declared that we were good. We are precious and honored in His eyes, for He has given men, even His own Son, as a ransom for the return of us to Him (Isaiah 43:4). Since we have so many conflicting images of what beauty should be in the world's eyes, we have to ask ourselves this question: Where do believers get their self-esteem?

The foundation of our self-esteem is based on Genesis 1:26. The scripture says we are created in the image and likeness of God, which is our spiritual resemblance. The likeness of our character is constantly being developed through sanctification; therefore, it makes us beautiful in any skin we are in. Our Genesis 1:26 image is the only image we should maintain.

If our likeness or image is of God, then we favor or mirror God's character. What is the character of God? What is His image? Well, as we have gone through our journey in holiness, faith and purity, we have examined God's character & image. The first sixteen days discussed what we needed to develop in our walk to become more like Him, and the last thirteen days identified issues that can affect our spiritual development.

None of this matter if we do not have the right foundation of faith and identity. We must believe God and know who we are in Him. Do we know who we really are?

We must put aside how our families, our roles, our jobs and the world define us. Yes, we are just like our daddies. We are made in the image of Him. Our confidence comes from Him, for we can only boast Christ and preach Him crucified. That is the core of who we are.

Neither our circumstances, our brokenness, our backgrounds nor our mistakes define us. How we handle them and how we choose to see them as classrooms for learning is what really matters. God is the sovereign Lord, and He determines who we are now and who we will become in the future.

Mephibosheth let a disability define who he was. When David searched for someone out of Jonathan's bloodline to bless, he found out about Mephibosheth. He tried to disqualify himself from David's blessing in 2 Samuel 9:8 (NIV), "Mephibosheth bowed down and said, 'What is your servant, that you should notice a dead dog like me?" He allowed the lameness in his feet to lower his self-esteem. Have you allowed something to lower your self-esteem?

When we base our identities and self-esteem in God, we will face whatever comes our way with the same declaration of Joshua and Caleb (Numbers 13:30): "Let us go up at once, and possess it; for we are well able to overcome it." Possess the identity God has given you, lift up your heads ye everlasting doors and let the King of Glory come in and shine through you. Seeing His glory come upon you----now that is real beauty!

Romans 12:3, 2 Corinthians 10:12, Ephesians 2:10

ᨑ *MY REFLECTIONS* ᨑ